GOSPEL SHAPED
LIVING

Handbook

GOSPEL SHAPED

LIVING

Vermon Pierre

THE GOSPEL
COALITION the good book
COMPANY

GOSPEL SHAPED LIVING

Gospel Shaped Living Handbook
© The Gospel Coalition / The Good Book Company 2015

Published by:
The Good Book Company
Tel (US): 866 244 2165
Tel (UK): 0333 123 0880
Email (US): info@thegoodbook.com
Email (UK): info@thegoodbook.co.uk

Websites:
North America: www.thegoodbook.com
UK: www.thegoodbook.co.uk
Australia: www.thegoodbook.com.au
New Zealand: www.thegoodbook.co.nz

ISBN: 9781909919273 Printed in the US

PRODUCTION TEAM:

AUTHOR:
Vermon Pierre

**SERIES EDITOR FOR
THE GOSPEL COALITION:**
Collin Hansen

**SERIES EDITOR FOR
THE GOOD BOOK COMPANY:**
Tim Thornborough

**MAIN TEACHING SESSION
DISCUSSIONS:** Alison Mitchell

DAILY DEVOTIONALS:
Carl Laferton

BIBLE STUDIES:
Tim Thornborough

EDITORIAL ASSISTANTS:
Jeff Robinson (TGC), Rachel Jones (TGBC)

VIDEO EDITOR:
Phil Grout

PROJECT ADMINISTRATOR:
Jackie Moralee

EXECUTIVE PRODUCER:
Brad Byrd

DESIGN:
André Parker

CONTENTS

 **PREFACE**

GROWING A GOSPEL SHAPED CHURCH

The Gospel Coalition is a group of pastors and churches in the Reformed heritage who delight in the truth and power of the gospel, and who want the gospel of Christ crucified and resurrected to lie at the center of all we cherish, preach and teach.

We want churches called into existence by the gospel to be shaped by the gospel in their everyday life.

Through our fellowship, conferences, and online and printed media, we have sought to encourage pastors and church leaders to calibrate their lives around what is of first importance—the gospel of Christ. In these resources, we want to provide those same pastors with the tools to excite and equip church members with this mindset.

In our foundation documents, we identified five areas that should mark the lives of believers in a local fellowship:

1. Empowered corporate worship
2. Evangelistic effectiveness
3. Counter-cultural community
4. The integration of faith and work
5. The doing of justice and mercy

We believe that a church utterly committed to winsome and theologically substantial expository preaching, and that lives out the gospel in these areas, will display its commitment to dynamic evangelism, apologetics, and church planting. These gospel-shaped churches will emphasize repentance, personal renewal, holiness, and the wonderful life of the church as the body of Christ. At the same time, there will be engagement with the social structures of ordinary people, and cultural engagement with art, business, scholarship and government. The church will be characterized by firm devotion to the truth on the one hand, and by transparent compassion on the other.

The Gospel Coalition believes in the priority of the local church, and that the local church is the best place to discuss these five ministry drivers and decide how to integrate them into life and mission. So, while being clear on the biblical principles, these resources give space to consider what a genuine expression of a gospel-shaped church looks like for you in the place where God has put you, and with the people he has gathered into fellowship with you.

Through formal teaching sessions, daily Bible devotionals, group Bible studies and the regular preaching ministry, it is our hope and prayer that congregations will grow into maturity, and so honor and glorify our great God and Savior.

Don Carson
President

Tim Keller
Vice President

INTRODUCTION

We have become used to a lot of things today—things we have come to accept as a normal part of living in our world.

We accept that conflict is just a part of daily life; and we accept that conflict between people will inevitably lead to division and dysfunction. We accept that people will be motivated by selfishness, and make choices based on their needs before considering the needs of others. We accept that people will tell lies and distort the truth to their own advantage. We accept that life will be a struggle, and will end in suffering and death. We have accepted that nasty is normal.

Yet at the same time, everyone instinctively senses that this is *just not right*. That life doesn't have to be this way; that things ought to be different. This may be normal life, but it isn't optimal life.

Christians are people who have discovered that something incredible has happened—something that broke through the walls built up around what we're used to and what our world accepts as normal. This "something" is that Jesus Christ rose from the dead. And because he rose, everything is different. Change, forgiveness and new life are now possible. A crack of light has broken into the darkness of the world. Division, dysfunction, selfishness and death do not have to be the final answer. Rather, by faith in Christ, we can now live the life of Christ.

And when Christians who are gathered together as the church live out this life within the world, they become a truly "counter-cultural community"—a community that still lives within the culture, but now shines with the light of a new culture, one shaped by and grounded in the gospel of Jesus Christ.

The Gospel Coalition has included this statement in their Theological Vision for Ministry, entitled "Counter-cultural community." It begins:

> *Because the gospel removes both fear and pride, people should get along inside the church who could never get along outside. Because it points us to a man who died for his enemies, the gospel creates relationships of service rather than of selfishness. Because the gospel calls us to holiness, the people of God live in loving bonds of mutual accountability and discipline. Thus the gospel creates a human community radically different from any society around it.*[1]

[1] You can read the full text of the statement on page 158

In this curriculum we will think through what it means for a church to be a counter-cultural community within the world. We won't do that by thinking primarily about culture, style or gimmicks—but about the gospel. We will see some of the principal ways in which a church that is being shaped by the gospel will live in stark contrast to the world around us; and how this will set it both at odds with its society, and yet also be strangely attractive to those in that society.

For example, what does it mean for the church to show unity in contrast to worldly divisions? What impact will it have when a self-centered world sees a church community that is full of sacrificial love and generosity? How can Christians hold to and speak out about truth in a way that is loving?

You might be unsettled as you work through this material and see significant areas where you and your church are still too much like the world, or too distant from the world. Don't give up or try to avoid what the Lord needs to reveal within you and your church. Instead, prayerfully work through these sessions with the happy and humble confidence that God wants to fill you even more with "the light of the gospel of the glory of Christ" (2 Corinthians 4:4). Trust that as this happens, many of the people you know and interact with day by day will begin to walk away from the darkness of sin and be drawn toward the light of the gospel.

Vermon Pierre

HOW TO USE GOSPEL SHAPED LIVING

MAIN TEACHING SESSION This session combines watching short talks on a DVD or listening to "live" talks with times for discussion. These prompt you to think about what you have heard and how it might apply to your church and cultural context. Bear in mind that there is not necessarily a "right answer" to every question!

DEVOTIONALS Each session comes with six daily personal devotionals. These look at passages that are linked to the theme of the Main Teaching Session, and are for you to read and meditate on at home through the week after the session. You may like to do them in addition to or instead of your usual daily devotionals, or use them to begin such a practice.

JOURNAL As you reflect on what you have learned as a group and in your personal devotionals, use this page to record the main truths that have struck you, things you need to pray about, and issues you'd like to discuss further or questions you'd like to ask.

BIBLE STUDY As part of this curriculum, your church may be running weekly Bible Studies as well as the Main Teaching Sessions. These look more closely at a passage and help you focus on an aspect of the Main Teaching Session. If your church is not using this part of the curriculum, you could work through it on your own or with another church member.

SERMON NOTES Your church's preaching program may be following this curriculum; space has been provided for you to make notes on these sermons in your Handbook.

SESSION 1:

YOUR CHURCH: A LIGHT IN THE DARKNESS

BOTH INSIDE AND OUTSIDE THE CHURCH, THERE ARE MANY DIFFERENT VIEWS OF WHAT A CHURCH ACTUALLY IS. IN THIS INTRODUCTORY SESSION, YOU'LL DISCOVER HOW GOD'S CHURCH IS MADE UP OF UNIQUE PEOPLE, WITH A UNIQUE PURPOSE. AND YOU'LL BEGIN TO SEE WHY GOD HAS PUT YOU IN YOUR CHURCH, AND WHY HE HAS PUT YOUR CHURCH WHERE HE HAS.

YOUR CHURCH: A LIGHT IN THE DARKNESS

Discuss

What do people who don't go to church think of Christians and the church?

_____

_____

_____

_____

▶ **WATCH DVD 1.1 OR LISTEN TO TALK 1.1**

_____

_____

_____

_____

_____

_____

_____

_____

_____

_____

_____

_____

_____

_____

Discuss

How do people treat the church as consumers? Do you ever find yourself doing this?

What unhelpful things does this lead to? What are people missing out on who treat their Christian faith in this way?

The church isn't just a community of Christians. It doesn't exist purely for the sake of the people who are in it. Instead, Jesus said that Christians are to stand out—to "shine" in a dark world:

☞ MATTHEW 5:14-16

[14] *You are the light of the world. A city set on a hill cannot be hidden.* [15] *Nor do people light a lamp and put it under a basket, but on a stand, and it gives light to all in the house.* [16] *In the same way, let your light shine before others, so that they may see your good works and give glory to your Father who is in heaven.*

Is Jesus' view of the local church bigger than yours? How?

▶ **WATCH DVD 1.2 OR LISTEN TO TALK 1.2**

_____

_____

_____

_____

_____

_____

_____

_____

Discuss

We are a unique people:

● Born again

● Adopted into a new family

● We have moved from light to darkness

● A new creation

● Having eternal life

The Bible uses these pictures, among others, to show how we become different when we respond to the gospel. Which of these descriptions excites you most? Why?

_____

_____

_____

_____

In 1 Peter 2:9, Peter says that God has called us "out of darkness into his marvelous light." Why is it so important that we do not forget what we have been saved from (the "darkness")?

_____

_____

_____

_____

_____

_____

▶ **WATCH DVD 1.3 OR LISTEN TO TALK 1.3**

_____

_____

_____

_____

_____

_____

_____

_____

_____

_____

_____

_____

Discuss

When Christians talk about being different than the world, they often focus on the things they do **not** do—getting drunk, watching porn on TV, stealing stationery from work, etc. What is the downside of this approach to thinking about our distinctiveness as believers?

_____

_____

_____

_____

_____

How would you describe Christian distinctiveness positively, but not proudly?

_____

_____

_____

_____

_____

Pray

This curriculum looks at the qualities and character that should mark our lives as we grow as believers.

Pray that as you all work through this curriculum, you will understand more deeply who we have been made in Christ, and that you will reflect this as a church family.

Pray that you will grow in the qualities listed above and, as a result, shine more brightly in the world around you.

DAILY BIBLE DEVOTIONALS

This week we'll look at 1 Peter 2:9-10, where the apostle Peter reaches back into the Old Testament to present us with a breathtaking description of who your church is.

Day 1

1 PETER 2:9; DEUTERONOMY 7:6-11

"You are a chosen race."

In Deuteronomy 7, God is speaking through Moses to the nation of Israel as they stand on the verge of the promised land.

Q: *What did God choose Israel to be (v 6)?*

Q: *What wasn't the reason for his choice (v 7)? What was the reason (v 8)?*

And as Peter writes to first-century people from a great variety of ethnic and religious backgrounds who have come to faith in Christ, he says: *This describes you.* Each local church is a gathering of God's chosen race; it is an expression of a new humanity that undercuts and supersedes all other allegiances.

And because, like Israel, we are selected not because of our performance, but because of God's promise, there is never any room for pride, nor need for anxiety; instead we live in humble confidence. We owe all we are and all we have to God's choice to love us; but we know that God *has* chosen to love us.

PRAY: *Almighty God, thank you that you love your people because you have chosen to, not because of our successes or failures. Give us a sense of humble confidence.*

Day 2

1 PETER 2:9; EXODUS 19:1-6

"You shall be … a kingdom of priests."

Within the kingdom of Israel, priests were to speak to God about the people, and talk to the people about God. Within the world, the role of this kingdom of priests—all Israel—was to pray to God for the salvation of the nations, and to talk to the nations about the saving God.

Now Peter says to the church: *You are this kingdom.* The job of King is taken—given by God to his Son, Jesus. The job of priests has been graciously given by God to… you and me. This is a weighty privilege. Priests represent God; therefore they will either promote or profane him. **Read Ezekiel 36:16-22.** Israel lurched between looking down on the nations and living just like the nations, but failed to show and speak of their God to the nations. Let the same not be said of us.

Q: *How might you, or your church, profane God in the way Israel did?*

Q: *What will it mean for you to be a priest, under the rule of King Jesus, today?*

PRAY: *Jesus, thank you for bringing me into your kingdom. Please show me how I can promote you, and reveal to me where I am in danger of profaning you.*

Day 3

1 PETER 2:9; EXODUS 19:1-6

"You are … a holy nation."

Q: *Read 1 Peter 1:14-17. How do we know what it means to "be holy"?*

Q: *How does knowing holiness is God-likeness motivate us to pursue it?*

Israel at Sinai (and the church today) is told to live, first and foremost, gazing upwards. We know there is a Judge of all, and yet we also know we call him Father (v 17). So we are to seek to grow in the likeness of our new family. And as we pursue holiness, we will be rejecting the ways of a world that seeks to be like God in authority, rather than like him in character. To be called to be holy is to be called to be different. The church will never find this easy; but it is intrinsic to our identity.

And yet, Israel at Sinai (and the church today) is called to live looking outwards, too. We are a nation in a world of nations. We are to learn to live among them in a way that makes our holy God real and wonderful to them. The church is called to be holy in a way that is invitational, not intimidating; embracing, not excluding. There is a border between the world and the church, and it is to be marked by holiness; and yet there should be no barriers or guards erected on the church's side of the border. The gospel is for all.

Q: *Is your church better at looking up, or out? How can you do both, better?*

PRAY: *Pray that your church will never forget to be holy, or to be active in the world.*

Day 4

1 PETER 2:9; DEUTERONOMY 26:16-19

"You are … a people for his own possession."

Q: *How does God see Israel (v 18)?*

Q: *What will this mean for them (v 19)?*

If you are familiar with the Old Testament, it is very easy to miss one of the most astonishing facts about it—from Genesis 12 onwards, its focus rests almost entirely on a single family, a nation nestled on the east of the Mediterranean Sea. God cares so deeply about, and invests his reputation so irreversibly in, the people of Israel that the story of his word is the story of this people.

Why? Because they are "his treasured possession." He owns and loves the world; but he *treasures* Israel. Imagine that: to live each day knowing that your nation is a treasure in the eyes of the Maker and Sustainer of every atom in existence and every hour of our lives.

Actually, you do not need to imagine—Peter looks at the church as he says: *You are a people for his own possession.* God brought us to himself through Christ so that he could treasure us. We could not be more loved, or looked out for, than we already are.

Q: *How can this change our thinking when we feel failures? Exhausted? Successful?*

Q: *How does your attitude toward your church compare with God's?*

PRAY: *Thank God for treasuring your church.*

Day 5

1 PETER 2:10; HOSEA 1:2-11

"Now you are God's people."

We have seen some awesome descriptions of Israel. But there was a problem. All of God's commitments to the people were conditional on their faithfulness and obedience to him. And throughout their history Israel would not, could not, keep those conditions.

Q: *How does God describe his people?*
- *Hosea 1:2* - *1:8-9*

Q: *But what does God promise (v 10)?*

God said to Israel: *You are not my people—no longer a chosen race, or kingdom of priests, a holy nation, my treasured possession.* But God also said *in* Israel: *You are my people, and I offer you all these blessings once more* (v 10). He did this when the only member of Israel to live a life of perfect, faithful obedience was forsaken by God—when the Lord Jesus, in his death, gave up all his privileges to bear the failings of God's people.

And so God now offers all people, everywhere, a place in his people, his church. And the wonder is that that entry is no longer conditional, but relational. It is available simply by appointing the perfect Israelite as our "head" (Hosea 1:11) and enjoying all the privileges that belong to him.

Q: *When was the last time you stopped to appreciate the chasm between what you deserve and what you have been given?*

PRAY: *Almighty God, impress upon my heart what it cost to make us your people.*

Day 6

1 PETER 2:9-10

These verses are almost all about what God has done for us in Christ, and about what his church is. There is only one mention of anything that we do...

Q: *God did all this for us "that you may..." what (v 9)?*

Q: *Why would doing this be a natural outworking of knowing:*
- *what the church is?*
- *what we were before we received mercy?*

Why does your church exist, where it is, in the time that it does, with the members it contains? Because God has placed it there, not to hold him tight so much as to hold him out. In all that we do, we are to show and share how excellent he is. A church should never point to itself or wag its finger at others. Rather, it should beckon all around to share the glories of being God's beloved people, with all that entails eternally. And we do this not because we have to, but because we want to; because it is who we are, and why we're here.

Q: *Meditate on each description of the church we have enjoyed this week. How has each one excited you about your faith, and your church?*

Q: *How has each one challenged you about your place in your church, and your church's life together?*

PRAY: *Turn each phrase of these verses into a prayer of thanks to God.*

 # JOURNAL

What I've learned or been particularly struck by this week…

_____

_____

_____

_____

_____

_____

What I want to change in my perspectives or actions as a result of this week…

_____

_____

_____

_____

_____

_____

Things I would like to think about more or discuss with others at my church…

_____

_____

_____

_____

_____

_____

JOURNAL

BIBLE STUDY

Discuss

Christians are called to be different. But we have often thought about our difference as being defined by the things we do *not* do. What are the advantages and disadvantages of this approach?

☞ READ LUKE 5:27-32

[31] *And Jesus answered them, "Those who are well have no need of a physician, but those who are sick.* [32] *I have not come to call the righteous but sinners to repentance."*

Tax collectors were hated by the Jews, as they were regarded as collaborators with the occupying Roman forces.

1. What is remarkable about what Jesus says and who he says it to?

_____

_____

_____

2. What is remarkable about Levi's response?

_____

_____

_____

What would it have cost Levi to follow Jesus?

_____

_____

_____

3. How do the Pharisees and teachers of the law respond (v 30)? What is behind their complaint, do you think?

_____

_____

_____

This incident reveals that the Jewish religious authorities are:

- *Legalistic*: They think that they get right with God by being obedient to the detailed laws of God—not by God's forgiving grace.
- *Separatist*: They believe that they must completely separate themselves from sinful people if they are to remain "pure."
- *Elitist*: They adopt a superior attitude toward "sinners," believing them to be of less value than themselves.

4. How does Jesus' response in verses 31-32 show them both who he is, and what he has come to do? How does his reply attack each of the three attitudes above?

_____

_____

_____

_____

5. How can we as a church fall into the same trap as the Pharisees and teachers of the law?

_____

_____

_____

6. How does Levi illustrate what our own focus should be in the Christian life?

_____

_____

7. Who are the "tax collectors and sinners" around your church? How might we be guilty of treating them as the Pharisees treat people in this story?

_____

_____

How can we be more welcoming to them, like Jesus, and more open to encouraging them, like Levi?

_____

_____

Apply

FOR YOURSELF: How are you living like Levi—in choosing to follow Jesus? When do you think you are most in danger of becoming a Pharisee in relation to your own holiness, and the sins of others? How will you help yourself and each other to avoid this?

_____

_____

_____

_____

FOR YOUR CHURCH: How "approachable" is your church to those who know they are sick and need a doctor? How might it feel like a club for holy people? How could it become more of a lifeboat for sinners?

_____

_____

_____

_____

Pray

FOR YOUR GROUP: Pray that you would grow as lights in the darkness as you work through this course together. Pray that the Lord would show you ways that you need to change and grow—and that he would give you the grace to do so.

FOR YOUR CHURCH: As your church embarks on this series examining what it means to be a shining light in the world, pray that you would grow together in seeing more clearly the light of the world—the Lord Jesus Christ—so that you will shine with his light in the darkness.

SERMON NOTES

Bible passage: Date:

_____

_____

_____

_____

_____

_____

_____

_____

_____

_____

_____

_____

_____

_____

_____

_____

_____

_____

_____

_____

SESSION 2:
A UNITED
CHURCH
IN A DIVIDED WORLD

DIVISION, MISUNDERSTANDING AND SEPARATION SEEM
INEVITABLE REALITIES IN THIS WORLD. SADLY, THEY ARE
ALSO OFTEN REALITIES WITHIN OUR CHURCHES. YET GOD'S
PEOPLE ARE CALLED TO BE DIFFERENT – TO BE UNITED.
HOW CAN WE ACHIEVE THIS WHEN OUR CHURCHES ARE
COLLECTIONS OF SELFISH SINNERS?

A UNITED CHURCH IN A DIVIDED WORLD

▶ WATCH DVD 2.1 OR LISTEN TO TALK 2.1

_____

_____

_____

_____

_____

_____

_____

_____

_____

_____

Discuss

Vernon gave a number of examples of division, separation and segregation, both in history and that exist today. What barriers between people are common in your local area?

_____

_____

_____

_____

_____

👉 **EPHESIANS 2:11-18**

> [11] Therefore remember that at one time you Gentiles in the flesh, called "the uncircumcision" by what is called the circumcision, which is made in the flesh by hands— [12] remember that you were at that time separated from Christ, alienated from the commonwealth of Israel and strangers to the covenants of promise, having no hope and without God in the world.
>
> [13] But now in Christ Jesus you who once were far off have been brought near by the blood of Christ. [14] For he himself is our peace, who has made us both one and has broken down in his flesh the dividing wall of hostility [15] by abolishing the law of commandments expressed in ordinances, that he might create in himself one new man in place of the two, so making peace, [16] and might reconcile us both to God in one body through the cross, thereby killing the hostility.
>
> [17] And he came and preached peace to you who were far off and peace to those who were near. [18] For through him we both have access in one Spirit to the Father.

Before we became Christians, what was our relationship with God, and with others?

v 12 _____

_____

_____

v 13 _____

v 14-15 _____

v 17 _____

v 18 (by implication) _____

What happens to those relationships when we are "in Christ"?

v 13 _____

v 14 _____

_____

v 15 _____

v 16 _____

_____

v 18 _____

▶ WATCH DVD 2.2 OR LISTEN TO TALK 2.2

_____

_____

_____

_____

_____

_____

_____

_____

_____

_____

_____

Discuss

Vermon said that "our broken *horizontal* relationships—with each other—ultimately come from a broken *vertical* relationship—with God." Can you think of some examples of this from your own situation?

_____

_____

_____

_____

Ephesians 2 tells us that, through the cross, Christians have been made into "one body" (v 16). What do you think that means?

_____

_____

_____

_____

_____

How does this show why disunity matters?

_____

_____

_____

_____

Ephesians 2 refers to Jews and Gentiles (non-Jews), but it applies much more widely than that. It tells us that the local church should be made up of the multiple ethnicities and/or social classes that are in the area. How does (or should) your church reflect your local area?

_____

_____

_____

_____

⏵ WATCH DVD 2.3 OR LISTEN TO TALK 2.3

_____

_____

_____

Discuss

What should we do when we are not united?

How can you put this into practice this week—as an individual, group or church?

Pray

"Unity among the different kinds of people within a local church is one of the most powerful witnesses we have of the truths of the gospel to our world."

Ask God to forgive you for any lack of unity in your church or group, or as individuals. Ask him to help you put into practice the things you listed above.

Pray that, as you do this, you and your church will be lights in a dark world, pointing to the reconciling work of God in your lives and the truth of the gospel message.

DAILY BIBLE DEVOTIONALS

How can we positively foster unity in our churches, as individual church members? Let Paul show you some very practical ways, as we work through Romans 12:9-21.

Day 1

ROMANS 12:9-21

Paul's main focus in v 9-13 is on our love for others within the church (see also v 4-8).

Q: *What should our love be (v 9)?*

Q: *How does the rest of verse 9 show what this means?*

True unity is founded on true love. And that love is "genuine"—literally, unhypocritical. We are to guard against a church culture where a sheen of politeness passes for "love" while covering over gossip, back-biting and malice.

The rest of v 9 shows that genuine love is willing to do and say hard things. It loves enough to challenge—to "abhor" it when we see someone failing God and themselves by sinning; to exhort them toward the "good." Hypocritical love never challenges because it is actually a love of being loved, not a love for another. How can we love genuinely? By finding our example of love in Christ's genuine love for us; and finding our identity not in being liked by others, but loved by him.

Q: *Are you genuinely loving? How/how not?*

PRAY: *Pray for this quality of love that none of us have naturally, but all of us can be given spiritually.*

Day 2

ROMANS 12:10

Q: *What are we to love each other "with"? (You will need to answer from the ESV.)*

Q: *Why do you think Paul uses familial language to describe the love God wants church members to show each other?*

In a good family, the family members enjoy ties that simply will not break, however different their lifestyles and decisions are. They spend time together, however great the geographical distances between them. They are doggedly committed to one another, making great sacrifices to honor and serve each other, without keeping score. Paul says: *Now you go treat your church like this.*

This challenges us, living in individualistic cultures. It may be hard for us, if we have experienced families that were (or are) hurtful. But this is also thrilling. If you never knew a good family, here is the family you yearn for. If you enjoyed a great family, here is the eternal family it was pointing you to.

Q: *Do you view, pray for, and treat your church with "brotherly affection"? Does anything need to change?*

PRAY: *Speak to God about your answer.*

Day 3

ROMANS 12:11-12

Q: What five things are we urged to do here?

Q: What do you understand each one to mean?

At first glance, these all seem to be about our own relationship with God—but remember that they come in a passage about how to be a loving, united church family. And failing in just one will hinder our church from shining in unity. We must not grow tired of caring deeply about one another as part of our service to the Lord (v 11). We are to rejoice when things go well within the church, be patient when things are hard, and pray when things go well *and* when they go badly!

It is very easy to cease to work at unity when church is how we want it to be and people are how we'd like them to be; it is very easy to lose our desire to work for unity when church is hard. It is always easier to forget to pray. It is always easier to hold back our hearts from others, rather than to be zealous and fervent and loving. Paul is telling us to be, and stay, emotionally invested in the lives of our brothers and sisters at church, because we are not just consumers using a mutually convenient service, nodding to one another and sharing a word or two. No—we are family, deeply involved with one another as we share life together. This is a mindset we'll only cultivate and keep by "constant ... prayer"!

Q: Which of these attitudes or behaviors do you most need to pray for and work at?

PRAY: Pray about each phrase in turn.

Day 4

ROMANS 12:13

Q: What two things does Paul tell us to do?

Q: In what ways do you find these hard to do, and to do joyfully? Why?

Love *does*. Love is not merely an idea or a feeling—it is practical action driven by a heart attitude. We discover whether we genuinely love others in the moment when it is costliest to love them. Your monthly bank statement will show you who you love most. Who has sat at your meal table this month will show you who you love most. In v 13, Paul says: *If you claim you love your church, have you put your money (and your house) where your mouth is?*

We follow a Lord who does not only speak love, but who does love. He did not come to teach us to love; rather, he came to die out of love. In Gethsemane, as he sweat blood (Luke 22:44), he walked toward the cross, because he loved us, and love does. At Calvary, as he shed blood, he stayed on the cross, because he loved us, and love does. If our love is not genuine—if it does not act for the good of others, at cost to ourselves in terms of money or time—then we need to gaze hard at the greatest love and the greatest cost the world has ever seen. Christ paid the ultimate price to welcome your church family into his heavenly home. What price could you bear for them, and what welcome could you share with them?

Q: How does this verse challenge you? How will Jesus' love motivate you?

PRAY: Pray that your love for others will be more like the Lord's love for you.

Day 5

ROMANS 12:14-16

These verses are a bridge between v 9-13, about loving unity within the church, and v 17-21, about loving humility beyond church. This part applies both in and out of the church.

Q: *What commands are we given here? Why are they difficult to live out in reality?*

Q: *When and how do you personally most struggle with each?*

Q: *How does obeying these verses mean a church family can "live in harmony"?*

Only the gospel enables us to live like this. When we are wronged and struggle to respond by blessing, we remember that we have wronged God far more than anyone has wronged us, and that he has shown us more undeserved blessing than we could ever extend to another. And we allow these truths to move us to "bless and … not curse" (v 14). When we find our greatest joy in Christ, we are able to enjoy others' blessings with them, even if they are blessings we would have liked; and we are able to mourn alongside them, even when that costs us emotion or energy (v 15). When we see ourselves in light of the gospel, we remember we have no reason for pride, and that it was not our intellectual insight that saved us (v 16). These three elements are critical for real unity; and they are possible only because of the gospel.

PRAY: *Spend time praising God for the gospel, and pray for areas, raised by these verses, where you need help to live it out.*

Day 6

ROMANS 12:17-21

Q: *What should we never do (v 17)?*

Q: *What should we seek to do (v 18)?*

Q: *Why do you think Paul adds "so far as it depends on you" in this verse?*

Q: *What truth enables us to give up our desire to avenge wrongs (v 19)?*

Revenge is a dish best served cold; and it is a dish best served by God, and not us. Because he is the Judge, we are not to be; and we do not need to be. Notice the other reason Paul gives for loving our enemy in v 20-21. If we repay evil with evil, evil wins; and the one who wronged us learns that this is the way to live in the world. If we repay evil with good, we have "overcome" evil—it hasn't infected us—and we show the one who wronged us that there is a different way to live—"dog feed dog" can replace "dog eat dog." The end of v 20 likely means to cause someone to repent—to admit their wrong and seek forgiveness. It is as we love our enemies that we offer people a glimpse of the greatest Lover of enemies: the One who hung on a cross and said of his executioners: "Father, forgive them" as he bore their sins (Luke 23:34).

Q: *Do you need, right now, to forgive someone who has wronged you, to stop seeking or imagining revenge, and actively to bless them?*

PRAY: *Re-read the whole of Romans 12:9-21, pausing at the end of each verse to turn it into both praise and prayer.*

 # JOURNAL

What I've learned or been particularly struck by this week…

_____

_____

_____

_____

_____

_____

What I want to change in my perspectives or actions as a result of this week…

_____

_____

_____

_____

_____

_____

_____

Things I would like to think about more or discuss with others at my church…

_____

_____

_____

_____

_____

_____

BIBLE STUDY

Discuss

Why do you think there are so many different Christian denominations? What is good about this variety? What is less good about it?

READ GENESIS 11:1-9

⁶ And the LORD said, "Behold, they are one people, and they have all one language, and this is only the beginning of what they will do. And nothing that they propose to do will now be impossible for them."

1. What unites the world that is pictured in verses 1-5?

_____

_____

_____

2. What lies behind why God confuses their language and scatters them? What would happen if they were not scattered?

_____

_____

_____

Ever since Babel, we have lived in a disunited world. In the Old Testament, the 12 tribes of Israel—made up from very different characters (see Genesis 49)—were saved together and united to serve the true and living God. But even they could not stay united—they broke apart into two kingdoms (1 Kings 12). *How would God's purposes of unity be fulfilled?*

We pick up the story on the Day of Pentecost after the events of the first Easter...

47

READ ACTS 2:1-13

⁵ Now there were dwelling in Jerusalem Jews, devout men from every nation under heaven. ⁶ And at this sound the multitude came together, and they were bewildered, because each one was hearing them speak in his own language.

3. Who was gathered in Jerusalem at this time (v 5-11)?

What did the Holy Spirit immediately enable Jesus' disciples to do?

What did they use this remarkable gift for (v 11, see also v 22-40)?

4. What is the implication of this in light of what we read in Genesis 11?

5. What are the implications of God's big plan for our view of the worldwide church (see also Acts 2:17-18)?

What are the implications of God's big plan for our view of "local" church (see also v 42-47)?

_____

_____

_____

_____

What are the implications of God's big plan for our view of local and international disputes and division?

_____

_____

_____

6. Why is such unity in diversity so attractive to outsiders? Have you seen this working in your own experience?

_____

_____

_____

_____

Sometimes our unity is shallow because our fellowship is shallow. We are able to maintain a theoretical unity because we do not intimately share our lives together. But when we are close to each other, the possibility for upset and disunity is much greater.

7. In your experience, what are some of the main obstacles to a genuine expression of warm, loving unity in the local church?

_____

_____

_____

_____

8. What do we need to remember when we face similar issues as a church?

_____

_____

_____

Apply

FOR YOURSELF: Which particular part of being united with your fellow believers do you struggle most with? What cultural barriers do you most struggle to get over? What aspect of the gospel message will help deal with this?

_____

_____

_____

_____

FOR YOUR CHURCH: How apparent to an outside observer is the unity in diversity that you have in Christ? What might need to change so that you have more opportunity to both practice and showcase this unity?

_____

_____

_____

Pray

FOR YOUR GROUP: Praise God together for the unity you have in Christ. Pray that you would remember the gospel that unites you, and work at the gritty realities of being united in your day-to-day experience.

FOR YOUR CHURCH: Ask the Lord to help your leaders when they are faced with particularly difficult or damaging disunity in the congregation. Pray that you would grow and develop ways to show your unity to a world that is hungry for it.

SERMON NOTES

Bible passage: Date:

SESSION 3:

A SERVING CHURCH

IN A SELFISH WORLD

WE LIVE IN A "ME ME ME" WORLD. WE TEND TO SEE, AND WANT, AND TAKE. YET OUR LORD CAME NOT TO BE SERVED, BUT TO SERVE, EVEN AT THE COST OF HIS OWN LIFE. IN THIS SESSION, YOU WILL BE ENCOURAGED AND CHALLENGED TO TAKE AS YOUR MODEL THE KING WHO SERVES, RATHER THAN OUR SELFISH WORLD – TO LIVE WITH A "YOU YOU YOU" MENTALITY.

A SERVING CHURCH IN A SELFISH WORLD

Discuss

You don't need to teach toddlers to be selfish—they naturally show the selfishness that is true of all of us. How have you seen that in small children, and in yourself?

_____

_____

_____

_____

_____

▶ WATCH DVD 3.1 OR LISTEN TO TALK 3.1

_____

_____

_____

_____

_____

_____

_____

_____

_____

_____

MATTHEW 20:20-28

[20] *Then the mother of the sons of Zebedee came up to him with her sons, and kneeling before him she asked him for something.* [21] *And he said to her, "What do you want?" She said to him, "Say that these two sons of mine are to sit, one at your right hand and one at your left, in your kingdom."* [22] *Jesus answered, "You do not know what you are asking. Are you able to drink the cup that I am to drink?" They said to him, "We are able."* [23] *He said to them, "You will drink my cup, but to sit at my right hand and at my left is not mine to grant, but it is for those for whom it has been prepared by my Father."*

[24] *And when the ten heard it, they were indignant at the two brothers.* [25] *But Jesus called them to him and said, "You know that the rulers of the Gentiles lord it over them, and their great ones exercise authority over them.* [26] *It shall not be so among you. But whoever would be great among you must be your servant,* [27] *and whoever would be first among you must be your slave,* [28] *even as the Son of Man came not to be served but to serve, and to give his life as a ransom for many."*

Discuss

What do you think was the motivation behind the request of James and John, the sons of Zebedee? Why might the other disciples have been so angry with them?

What, by contrast, is Jesus' definition of "greatness" in the kingdom of God (v 25-28)? Why would the disciples have found this hard to swallow? Why do we?

How is Jesus a perfect example of self-sacrifice for us?

_____

_____

_____

_____

▶ WATCH DVD 3.2 OR LISTEN TO TALK 3.2

_____

_____

_____

_____

_____

_____

_____

_____

Discuss

"The church is to be radically and shockingly different to our culture in that they are a people willing to give up their whole lives for the good of others."

Share two or three very practical examples of how we can show this kind of sacrifice with our time, money or gifts. How will our natural selfishness prevent us from serving others in these ways?

_____

_____

_____

_____

"The church stands out within a self-serving world by being a community of self-sacrificing love." How do you see this happening in your own church family? Are there areas that could be improved upon?

_____

_____

_____

How does the gospel enable us to give our lives up for others?

_____

_____

_____

▶ WATCH DVD 3.3 OR LISTEN TO TALK 3.3

_____

_____

_____

_____

_____

_____

_____

_____

Discuss

Sacrifice is hard! Why do we need to keep reminding ourselves that this is true?

_____

_____

"When we serve others sacrificially, what we give is reinvested by God into the lives of others." How have you seen this happen, as an individual or church?

What does selfishness look like in a church? How can you avoid this?

Pray

"Jesus, the leader of all leaders, the Son of God, the Lord of the universe, sets himself as an example of this for his followers: '... even as the Son of Man came not to be served but to serve' (Matthew 20:28)."

Spend some time praising Jesus for his immense self-sacrifice in coming to live as a man, so that he could die for our sins.

Ask God to help you become more like Jesus, so that your lives show the same love and self-sacrifice to those around you.

DAILY BIBLE DEVOTIONALS

When we read a Gospel with our focus on learning about service, we find Jesus giving us both model and motivation. We serve as those who have already been served.

Day 1

LUKE 7:11-17

Q: *Who is this woman burying (v 12)? Who else has she already buried?*

Q: *How does Jesus serve her (v 14-15)? What causes him to do this (v 13)?*

"Compassion" literally means that Jesus' bowels moved within him—he had a gut reaction to this tragic scene (the NIV translates it as: "His heart went out to her"). How Jesus *felt* drove what Jesus *did*. He never settled for brokenness, or grew indifferent to others' suffering—he identified with them and entered into their lives. He ached for them.

Q: *To what extent is this your response to those whose lives have been broken?*

Service always involves sacrifice. But what does Jesus risk or give here? He "touched the bier" (or coffin). Such contact with the dead left someone unclean, outside God's people (Numbers 5:2). Jesus does not only identify with the woman's grief; he enters into the uncleanness and exclusion of her son's death, to bring life and inclusion. As he touches death to bring life to this man, we glimpse the moment he tasted death to bring life to us.

PRAY: *Pray that you would share Jesus' ache for the hurting and broken.*

Day 2

LUKE 8:22-25

Q: *What does Jesus do on the boat (v 23a)?*

The Gospel of Matthew fills in the details of these 24 hours of Jesus' life. He had taught his great "Sermon on the Mount" (Matthew 5 – 7); he had healed many people (8:1-17); he had challenged a scribe who thought following him would be easy (8:18-22). Still ahead of him lay a confrontation with demons, a debate with religious leaders, and a dealing with death (8:28 – 9:26). We can imagine how exhausted he must have been, and how much he needed a rest on the boat.

Q: *What was Jesus still ready to do (Luke 8:24)?*

Of course we are not the Son of God. We are not able to calm the storm for our friends—neither the storms of life, nor the storm of judgment at the end of life. But we do face moments when we are feeling tired, and the choice comes: *sleep or serve?* We are not never to rest; but we are to be willing to give up our relaxation for others' good—and enjoy living like, and reflecting, Jesus as we do so.

Q: *How and when do you face this choice?*

PRAY: *Thank Jesus he is with you through the storms, even through death; and ask for energy to serve when weary.*

Day 3

LUKE 8:40-56

Q: *Which two people does Jesus help? Which one had the influential father?*

Q: *Why do you think Jesus stopped to speak to the already-healed woman (v 44-47)? What did he want to say to her (v 48)?*

There was huge value for Jesus' reputation and mission in going to Jairus' house to heal his daughter. This was a man with status, respected in his town. But there was nothing to be gained from healing, and stopping to speak with, a lady whose 12-year illness had left her penniless and unclean (see Leviticus 15:25). In fact, by stopping, Jesus risked Jairus' displeasure and disapproval, since the delay meant the daughter died (Luke 8:49).

But Jesus did not only come to speak with and serve the important, to help when he might get something out of helping. He came for "little people"—the unnoticed, inconsequential and rejected. Nobody is a nobody to him. So it must be for us. We deserve an eternity of rejection… and Jesus came for us. We must not limit our help to those who can give back, or whose approval we pragmatically decide will help our mission.

How do you treat the "little people" around you, inside and outside church? That will tell you much about how well you know Jesus.

Q: *How does this both encourage and challenge you?*

PRAY: *Thank Jesus for serving even you. Pray that you will notice, make time for, and serve the "little people," as he did.*

Day 4

Jesus shows us what a life of service looks like. He also warns about what a life of selfishness leads to.

LUKE 12:13-21

Q: *What causes Jesus to tell this parable?*

Q: *Imagine you had lived next door to this man. How sensible would his decisions have seemed? How might you have envied him?*

Q: *What is God's verdict on the man in the parable (v 20)? Why?*

Who were the rich man's bigger barns for? Himself. It was all about "I" and "my." His life was about getting and enjoying. His use of his wealth reveals his heart. But in seeking to keep everything, he lost everything.

How different the attitude, and future, of the One telling the story! He had given up heaven's riches in order to come and teach and warn. He was on his way to Jerusalem, where he would give up his life in order to rescue and restore. In this sense, Jesus never said "I" or "my"—his life was lived for, and given for, others. His use of his wealth revealed his heart.

It is possible to be saved, but to live as a fool. But it is so much better, eternally, to live as a servant. **Read Luke 19:17.**

Q: *Which verdict from the Lord would your life draw—the one of 19:17, or of 12:20?*

PRAY: *Thank Jesus for giving up so much to build a home in eternity for you. Ask him to show you how to live as a servant, not a fool— and help you make any changes you need to.*

Day 5

LUKE 13:10-17; 14:1-6

Q: *What is so controversial about these two healings (13:14)?*

Q: *How does the Lord Jesus respond to this controversy (13:15-16; 14:3-5)?*

Jesus' opponents, who are "watching him carefully" (14:1), in order to try to trap him into doing or saying something they can use to accuse or discredit him, are left ashamed (13:17) and silenced (14:6)—and hating him even more, exposed as they are as hypocrites.

Q: *Why was offending and alienating these people risky?*

Don't miss the decision that Jesus is making in episodes such as these. It is easy to assume that he would heal these people, because we are so used to his servant-heartedness. But Jesus can only heal them if he adds further ink to his own charge sheet. None of us like to be hated. None of us like to stand up to power. Many of us allow our deeds to be directed by our own popularity and safety. Jesus never did. He did what was right, not what was easy.

Q: *Can you think of times in your own life when to serve people by speaking truth or doing good also involves causing offense or risking dislike?*

When serving others requires giving up popularity or risking safety, know that your Lord has trodden this path, calls you to do the same, and is delighted when you do.

PRAY: *Ask Jesus to help you love others more than your own ease or safety.*

Day 6

LUKE 21:1-4

Q: *In God's economy, why are two small coins worth more than great gifts?*

Q: *How does this encourage us when we feel we do not have much to give?*

Perhaps you do not have as much time, health, energy, wealth, or insight as others. But Jesus does not weigh your service against what others can do, but according to what *you* can. He asks you simply to give what you can. And he notices and cares about it whenever you do. We can imagine him looking from heaven, noticing a child of his giving all they can, unnoticed by those around them, and saying to his angels: *Look at him. Look at her. Look how they give, how they serve. I'm delighted!*

And in asking us to give what we have, Jesus is not asking for anything he has not done...

LUKE 22:39-46

Q: *How is Jesus feeling here? What does he want (v 42)?*

"This cup" is the cup of God's wrath (Isaiah 51:17), which fits our sinful hands, but which Christ would take in his perfect hands and drink on our behalf. Here, he recoils from it in horror. But he resolves to take hold of it. Why? Because he loves his Father, and he loves his people. He has given you more, and given up more, than you will ever give for him.

Q: *How does this move you to worship him, and motivate you to serve like him?*

PRAY: *Thank Jesus for all he gave to serve you; pray for opportunities to give to serve him.*

JOURNAL

What I've learned or been particularly struck by this week…

_____

_____

_____

_____

_____

What I want to change in my perspectives or actions as a result of this week…

_____

_____

_____

_____

_____

Things I would like to think about more or discuss with others at my church…

_____

_____

_____

_____

_____

BIBLE STUDY

Discuss

Who have been your greatest role models for the Christian life? What was it about them that you found attractive and challenging?

READ PHILIPPIANS 2:1-30

¹ *So if there is any encouragement in Christ, any comfort from love, any participation in the Spirit, any affection and sympathy,* ² *complete my joy by being of the same mind, having the same love, being in full accord and of one mind.*

In this famous passage we see how the good news of the gospel leads to people who are united in Christ and willing to follow his example of sacrificial service.

1. What four things that come to us through the gospel does Paul point to in verse 1? How should each of these lead to the unity described in verse 2?

_____

_____

_____

_____

2. How should Christians treat each other (verses 3 and 4)?

_____

_____

_____

What stops us from doing this?

_____

_____

3. In verses 5-11 Jesus is revealed as God, as our Servant King, and as reigning in triumph. He chose to be born as a human being so that he could die on the cross in our place. How does this make you feel?

_____

_____

_____

4. How do verses 6-8 show us what it means to have Christ's "mind"?

_____

_____

_____

5. How does Jesus' humble, serving sacrifice for us transform the commands we are given in verses 12-18?

_____

_____

_____

Where does the strength come from to obey God's will in these ways?

_____

_____

_____

6. Look at the examples of Paul (v 17-18); Timothy (v 19-22); and Epaphroditus (v 25-30). How do each of these men model for us what it means to sacrifice ourselves for others?

_____

_____

_____

_____

_____

_____

_____

Which of these qualities would you like to grow more deeply in yourself?

_____

_____

_____

This curriculum is called *Gospel Shaped Living*. This chapter of Philippians shows how our new life and our lifestyle as believers are rooted in, inspired by and flow from the gospel of Christ crucified, who now reigns triumphant.

7. What are some practical steps suggested in this passage that we can take to grow more like Christ?

_____

_____

_____

_____

_____

Apply

FOR YOURSELF: Which of the steps you listed in Question 7 do you most need to focus on at the moment? How can this Bible-study group help you to do that?

_____

_____

_____

_____

FOR YOUR CHURCH: How can you help each other not to be trapped by grumbling and disputation? How can you encourage each other to leave aside selfish ambition and conceit?

_____

_____

_____

_____

Pray

FOR YOUR GROUP: Spend some time praising the Lord Jesus for his amazing sacrifice for us. Pray that you would honor him by the way you live—following his mindset of love and care for others, and his willingness to serve us.

FOR YOUR CHURCH: Pray that you would love each other more deeply—as Jesus loved us. Pray that you would increasingly encourage each other to shine like stars in the world.

SERMON NOTES

Bible passage: Date:

SESSION 4:

A GENEROUS CHURCH

IN A STINGY WORLD

THE GREAT REFORMER MARTIN LUTHER ONCE SAID THAT
THE LAST PLACE A MAN IS CHANGED BY THE GOSPEL IS IN
HIS WALLET. FIVE HUNDRED YEARS LATER, THAT IS STILL
TRUE. OUR BANK STATEMENTS SHOW MUCH ABOUT HOW
DEEPLY WE HAVE GRASPED THE GOSPEL. WONDERFULLY,
WHAT WE DO WITH OUR MONEY CAN ALSO HAVE A
GREAT IMPACT FOR THE GOSPEL. SO HOW DOES, AND HOW
SHOULD, THE GOSPEL SHAPE YOUR FINANCES?

A GENEROUS CHURCH IN A STINGY WORLD

Discuss

Imagine if we started this session by asking each person to tell the group how much they give to the church. Would you want to answer the question? Why / why not?

_____

_____

_____

_____

_____

▶ WATCH DVD 4.1 OR LISTEN TO TALK 4.1

_____

_____

_____

_____

_____

_____

_____

_____

_____

_____

Discuss

"On average, Christians only give a little over $2 for every $100 they earn." Does this surprise you? Why / why not?

_____

_____

_____

_____

What are some of the excuses we give ourselves for not being more generous with our money and time?

_____

_____

_____

_____

What are some of the wrong motives we can have for giving?

_____

_____

_____

_____

▶ WATCH DVD 4.2 OR LISTEN TO TALK 4.2

_____

_____

_____

_____

_____

_____

_____

_____

👉 READ 2 CORINTHIANS 8:1-7

[1] We want you to know, brothers, about the grace of God that has been given among the churches of Macedonia, [2] for in a severe test of affliction, their abundance of joy and their extreme poverty have overflowed in a wealth of generosity on their part. [3] For they gave according to their means, as I can testify, and beyond their means, of their own accord, [4] begging us earnestly for the favor of taking part in the relief of the saints— [5] and this, not as we expected, but they gave themselves first to the Lord and then by the will of God to us. [6] Accordingly, we urged Titus that as he had started, so he should complete among you this act of grace. [7] But as you excel in everything—in faith, in speech, in knowledge, in all earnestness, and in our love for you—see that you excel in this act of grace also.

Discuss

How is "generous grace" a good description of the Macedonian church?

_____

_____

_____

_____

Why are these two words inseparable as we think about this subject?

_____

_____

_____

_____

_____

We often find it especially hard to give to people who we think are undeserving. How does the gospel help us with this?

_____

_____

_____

_____

_____

▶ WATCH DVD 4.3 OR LISTEN TO TALK 4.3

_____

_____

_____

_____

_____

_____

_____

_____

Discuss

Many churches have an annual Sunday when they focus on giving, after which we tend to ask ourselves: "How much should I give?" What difference would it make if we asked instead: "How much can I give?"

_____

_____

_____

_____

What has God given you an abundance of (ie: more of than you need), which you can share with others?

_____

_____

_____

_____

"We should stand out as an island of generosity in a sea of stinginess." What will this look like for you as individuals? And as a church?

_____

_____

_____

_____

What changes are you going to make as a result of this session?

_____

_____

_____

_____

Pray

"Jesus lost everything so we could gain everything." Spend some time praising Jesus for his generosity to you, although you did not deserve it.

Ask God to help you become more like Jesus, so that you show generous grace to those around you.

Ask him to help your church to stand out as "an island of generosity."

DAILY BIBLE DEVOTIONALS

Martin Luther said the last place where conversion makes a difference is the wallet. We are focusing on our wallets this week, as we work through 2 Corinthians 8 – 9.

Day 1

2 CORINTHIANS 8:1-9

Q: *What do you find most surprising, and challenging, about the example of the churches of Macedonia (v 2-4)?*

It is relatively easy to settle for being willing to give sacrificially. But it is another thing entirely to be *wanting* to give sacrificially. Yet that is the sign of an individual or a church that has truly been given, and has deeply grasped, "the grace of God" (v 1).

Q: *Who had the Macedonian churches given themselves to (v 5)? How does this explain why they wanted to give?*

Q: *These churches clearly knew the truth of verse 9. So would they have seen themselves as poor, or rich, or both?*

We need to learn to look at our bank balance through gospel lenses. Whether our account is overflowing or almost empty, we are no more or less rich—for we have been given eternal, heavenly riches in Christ. When you give your money sacrificially, you are giving a cent away, compared to the million dollars stored in your heavenly bank account. And as you give, you are acting like, and becoming like, Jesus. Do you know this? Then you will want to give.

PRAY: *Lord, help me want to give. Amen.*

Day 2

2 CORINTHIANS 8:10-15

Q: *What had the Corinthian church started doing a year before, and why (v 10)?*

Q: *But what do they still need to do (v 11)?*

We live out our greatest desires. So if we say we desire to give, but don't, it means that an opposing desire—perhaps for security or comfort—is stronger. As God tells us how to use money, it is easy to say we want to give—but far harder to get on with it. Theory is not practice. Good intentions help no one.

Q: *Do you need to turn intention into action? How? Will you?*

Q: *How does v 12 encourage those with little, and challenge those with much?*

"How much should I give?" is always the wrong question. If we know, deep in our hearts, the grace of our Lord (v 9), we ask: "How much *can* I give?" The answer will vary from person to person and year to year. We are not to give in a way that leaves us needing to receive others' giving (v 13); we are to give in a way that means going without ourselves.

PRAY: *Lord, help me to know how much of what you have given me you wish me to give away. Then enable me to do it. Amen.*

Day 3

2 CORINTHIANS 8:16 – 9:5

Q: Who is Paul sending to collect the Corinthians' contribution to the financial gift he is gathering (v 16-19, 22-23)?

Q: Whose opinion does Paul care about when it comes to how the money is collected (v 21)?

What we give matters. Why we give matters. And how we give matters, too. Paul does not only want to do the right thing, and call this church to do the right thing; he wants to be seen to do the right thing.

Very little shipwrecks a church quicker than accusations of financial impropriety. Fresh air is the best disinfectant, and transparency the most effective defense. Paul was giving three useful gospel workers over to the task of ensuring the collection of the gift was done in a way that could withstand public scrutiny.

Paul then turns to encourage the church once again to turn intentions into action (9:2-3).

Q: What will happen if some generous Macedonians turn up with Paul, and the Corinthians haven't given anything (v 4)?

Imagine your church had a visit from some brothers and sisters from an impoverished church in the developing world who were giving sacrificially and joyfully. Would you be ashamed of your giving, or happy with it?

PRAY: Lord, please help us not only to do the right thing as a church, but to be seen to do it. Give us wisdom and honesty. And give us grace to get on with it. Amen.

Day 4

2 CORINTHIANS 9:6-11

Q: What is "the point" (v 6)? If we believed this, how would it affect our giving?

Q: What is God able to do (v 8)? What is his purpose in doing this (end v 8, end v 10, v 11)?

What do you trust to provide you with what you need today, tomorrow and the day after? Where do you look for "sufficiency"? If it is to God, we will radically obey, and we will cheerfully give. This is why God loves a willing, "cheerful," sacrificial giver (v 7), because that is concrete evidence of a person who trusts him to provide what they need, today and eternally. And that is a matter that is between us and God—a transaction we settle in our hearts, not that we trumpet before others.

There is nothing wrong with pension plans, insurance policies and so on—if they are invested in with the aim of us not becoming a burden later in life (8:12-13). But there is everything wrong with these things if they are what we trust to provide for us. Some of us need to be wiser in stewardship; most of us need to be more trusting, and therefore more giving. All of us need to seek a harvest of righteousness in our lives more than we aim for a glut of possessions or a secure financial future.

Q: Do you believe that God can give you all you need? How does that show in your bank statements?

PRAY: Lord, give me such trust in the gospel that I give sacrificially **and** cheerfully. Amen.

Day 5

2 CORINTHIANS 9:12-14

Paul now talks about the *results* of Christian giving to other Christians, as he outlines what will happen when the Corinthian collection reaches the poorer Jerusalem churches.

Q: *What two things will the Corinthians' giving cause (v 12)?*

Only if we have grasped the gospel will we be excited about this. In the gospel, we meet a God who rightly demands our praise because he is Creator; who doubly deserves our praise because he is our Redeemer; and who has saved us in order that we might please and praise him as our Father. Now, Paul says, when we give money away, we are actually buying not only help for our family, but also thanksgiving for our Father. Spend money on yourself and you buy only comfort for yourself. Give money to other Christians and you purchase praise for your glorious God.

Q: *How does this cause you to want to beg "earnestly for the favor of taking part in the relief of the saints" (8:4)?*

Q: *What two things will the recipients of giving be prompted to do (9:14)?*

Giving and receiving between churches strengthens our family ties. Our money flowing between people who will never meet till eternity is a great statement of our identity as brothers and sisters.

PRAY: *Creator, Redeemer and Father, I desire to praise you, and that others praise you. Thank you that I can use the money you have given me to this end. Amen.*

Day 6

2 CORINTHIANS 9:15

Throughout these chapters, Paul has been talking about Christians *like* us giving up what would be easiest or most pleasurable *for* us in order to give our money away to those who in this life will never *meet* us and who are in no position ever to *repay* us.

Q: *How does Paul describe having the opportunity to give in this way?*

It is a description that only the gospel can make sense of! Giving is not a chore, it is a joy; not a burden, but a gift. As we understand 2 Corinthians 8 and 9 in our heads, and as the Spirit presses it deep into our hearts, we won't be able to express how excited and grateful we are to be able to give our wealth away so that others might benefit from it.

This is counter-cultural in our society, and counter-instinctive for our hearts. So it is good to rehearse the reasons why we should, can and will give sacrificially and joyfully:

- 8:9
- 8:12
- 9:6, 8, 11
- 9:12
- 9:14a

Q: *How has your attitude toward giving been changed or reinforced by these devotionals?*

Q: *How will that attitude show itself in your actions regarding your finances?*

PRAY: *Lord, I long to see my giving as an inexpressible gift from you, to me. Please help me to live like this, and to give like this. Show me if anything needs to change in order for my accounts to better reflect my faith. Amen.*

JOURNAL

What I've learned or been particularly struck by this week...

_____

_____

_____

_____

_____

_____

What I want to change in my perspectives or actions as a result of this week...

_____

_____

_____

_____

_____

_____

Things I would like to think about more or discuss with others at my church...

_____

_____

_____

_____

_____

BIBLE STUDY

Discuss

Think about someone you might describe as a "generous person"—what qualities do they have that earn them your respect?

Where do you think their generosity comes from—is it their upbringing, their disposition, their circumstances or something else?

In this Bible study, we are going to look at a famous encounter with Jesus in Luke's Gospel.

READ LUKE 19:1-10

9 And Jesus said to him, "Today salvation has come to this house, since he also is a son of Abraham. 10 For the Son of Man came to seek and to save the lost."

1. What is the evidence in the passage that Zacchaeus was considered to be an outcast from the kingdom of God?

Why had he given up his reputation?

2. What does the way in which Zacchaeus seeks Jesus tell us about him?

3. How does this story show us the pattern of the gospel: God's grace toward undeserving sinners?

4. How does Zacchaeus' statement in verse 8 reveal the depth and reality of his response to the gospel invitation?

What had changed him from a money grabber to a money giver?

5. What advice would you give to a new Christian who asked you about what they should do with their money?

6. How will the love of money always remain a temptation for Christians? How can we prevent it from ensnaring us?

_____

_____

_____

_____

Apply

FOR YOURSELF: Where do you look for security, satisfaction and significance? How can you help yourself look to Jesus instead?

_____

_____

_____

_____

Generosity will always involve money, but it is about so much more than money. What has God made you rich in that you can be more generous with?

_____

_____

_____

_____

FOR YOUR CHURCH: How can you as a church better express the generous grace God has shown to you in your congregational life?

_____

_____

_____

_____

Pray

FOR YOURSELF: Ask God to help you be discerning about the false motives that may take root in your heart. Ask God to fill you with a sense of his generosity to you in the gospel—so that you will be generous to others. Pray that you would find someone who is in need of your generosity—and that you would be prepared to give yourself to them.

FOR YOUR CHURCH: Pray that God would make you a grateful fellowship, and that you would abound in thanksgiving. Ask God to help your leaders know how to encourage generosity in the life of the church. Pray that any visitors would be impacted by the generous grace they see and receive from your church.

SERMON NOTES

Bible passage: Date:

_____

_____

_____

_____

_____

_____

_____

_____

_____

_____

_____

_____

_____

_____

_____

_____

_____

_____

_____

_____

_____

SESSION 5:

A TRUTHFUL CHURCH

IN A CONFUSED WORLD

IN THE POSTMODERN WESTERN WORLD, TRUTH IS IN
SHORT SUPPLY — AND CONFIDENCE IN THE TRUTH IS
SCARCE, TOO. THIS SESSION CALLS US BACK TO A
ROBUST TRUST IN GOD'S TRUTH, REVEALED IN HIS SON,
PARTICULARLY IN AREAS WHERE TO LIVE BY HIS TRUTH IS
CONTROVERSIAL OR EVEN OFFENSIVE. BUT IT WILL ALSO
HELP US TO THINK THROUGH HOW WE COMMUNICATE
THAT TRUTH IN A WAY THAT HONORS HIS SON.

A TRUTHFUL CHURCH IN A CONFUSED WORLD

▶ WATCH DVD 5.1 OR LISTEN TO TALK 5.1

_____

_____

_____

_____

_____

_____

_____

_____

_____

_____

_____

Discuss

Can you think of an example from your own life of being in a fog of confusion that was changed by the truth of the gospel?

_____

_____

_____

_____

What are some of the main areas where your culture diverges from Christian views and in which Christians find themselves increasingly in conflict? How has this changed over the years?

_____

_____

_____

_____

"Jesus doesn't just tell the truth—he is the truth." What do you think this means?

_____

_____

_____

_____

Why it is wonderful that Jesus is full of *both* grace *and* truth?

_____

_____

_____

_____

▶ WATCH DVD 5.2 OR LISTEN TO TALK 5.2

_____

_____

_____

_____

Discuss

"Jesus is full of grace and truth—what he says is right and loving." How does knowing this help us answer the following accusations?

- Christianity is outdated

- Christianity is intolerant

- Christianity is judgmental

- Christianity is one view among many

- Christianity is oppressive

"Truth is not a battle we win merely by making a better argument. It is a battle we win by living a better life." What would this look like for you as an individual? And as a church?

_____

_____

_____

_____

▶ WATCH DVD 5.3 OR LISTEN TO TALK 5.3

_____

_____

_____

_____

_____

_____

_____

_____

_____

_____

EPHESIANS 4:15-16, 25

¹⁵ Rather, speaking the truth in love, we are to grow up in every way into him who is the head, into Christ, ¹⁶ from whom the whole body, joined and held together by every joint with which it is equipped, when each part is working properly, makes the body grow so that it builds itself up in love.

²⁵ Therefore, having put away falsehood, let each one of you speak the truth with his neighbor, for we are members one of another.

Discuss

What is the difference between "putting away falsehood" and "speaking the truth"?

What do you think it means to speak "the truth in love" (v 15)? When do we find this particularly hard to do? Or to hear?

What goes wrong when we (as individuals and as churches) speak the truth lovelessly? Or when we seek to love others but without speaking truth? Can you think of examples from your own experience of these two equal and opposite errors? Which do you tend toward personally?

Pray

"The light shines in the darkness, and the darkness has not overcome it" (John 1:5). Spend some time praising Jesus for being the true light.

Thank God for bringing you to know him through the light of the gospel.

Ask him to help you put into practice the things you discussed in this session.

DAILY BIBLE DEVOTIONALS

"In the past our culture largely bought into the Christian view on sex and marriage—but that's now rapidly falling away." This week, we focus on that Christian view.

Day 1

1 THESSALONIANS 4:1-2

Why obey God? If it is primarily so life will go better for you, it's actually selfish. If it is to earn God's blessings now or life in eternity, it's still selfish. And God is not pleased by that. It is possible to be obedient to God, yet anger God (**read Amos 5:21**). Motivation matters.

But here, we are pointed to another motivation. Paul writes to "you in the Lord Jesus" (1 Thess 4:1), reminding us that those who trust Christ share his relationship with his Father, as his beloved children. **Read Romans 8:8-17**. And as his children, they can now live in a way that brings him pleasure—they can "walk … to please God" (1 Thess 4:1).

From verse 3, Paul will be focusing on love, sex and relationships. And as his words equip and challenge you, remember: you can bring pleasure to your Father by trusting his Son and living by his commands. Let that motivate obedience!

Q: *Is your obedience wrongly motivated?*

Q: *How will the truth that you can bring pleasure to God through your obedience change your attitudes and actions today?*

PRAY: *Father, help me please you by obeying Jesus today, even when it is hard.*

Day 2

1 THESSALONIANS 4:3

Q: *What is the will of God (v 3a)?*

That is, to be holy, pure, like him. He has given us a holy status through Jesus' death; now, he works to grow us into holy people.

Q: *What is one way to be sanctified (v 3b)?*

Paul does *not* say "abstain from sex." He even tells us elsewhere not to abstain from talking about sex, but rather, to speak of it with "thanksgiving" (Ephesians 5:4). We should not be scared of sex, or of talking about it. God designed and celebrates sex (read Song of Solomon!). We must not make too little of sex by refusing to mention it, celebrate it, enjoy it.

But Paul *does* say we must not make too much of sex by viewing it as a must-have for fulfillment—as an idol. We are to keep it within the relationship God designed it for—a lifelong, complete commitment between a man and a woman (Gen. 2:22-25): marriage. When it comes to sex, our aim can be, and must be, to please God, and grow to be more like him, by avoiding sexual immorality.

Q: *How can you, in your specific circum-stances, please God with your sex life?*

PRAY: *Lord, show me how not to make too little of sex, nor too much of it, in my life.*

Day 3

1 THESSALONIANS 4:4

This is a hard verse to translate: but it's likely that "possess his own vessel" (see footnote) is talking of living well with a wife—and, by extension, living well with a husband.

Q: *What two words does Paul use to characterize the ideal sexual relationship between husband and wife?*

What does a sex life marked by "holiness" look like? Throughout Scripture, it is God who epitomizes holiness; God's character defines holiness. And central to his character is self-giving compassion; compassion is intrinsic to holiness. So Paul is saying: *Let your sex lives reflect the nature of the holy, compassionate, sacrificial God. Let your thoughts and actions be directed by what is best for the other.* Holy love never says: *It's time to put me first.* It never says: *My feelings are more important than yours.* It never says: *You have disappointed me one too many times, and I deserve more, so I am going elsewhere.* Holy love is both spouses committing to serve the other thoughtfully, compassionately, totally—in exactly the way our holy God serves us.

Q: *If you are married, is your love characterized by holiness? How, and how not? Could you ask your spouse today: "How can I love you in a more holy way?"*

Q: *If you are single, how can you love others with "holiness"—and so please God?*

PRAY: *Pray for marriages and singleness in your church, including yours—for growing holiness and honor to shine forth from them.*

Day 4

1 THESSALONIANS 4:5

There is another approach to sexuality, which is directed by another approach to the divine.

Q: *How do "Gentiles" (or "pagans") view their sex lives, does Paul say?*

Q: *How does Paul describe the Gentiles' relationship to God?*

By "lust," Paul means selfish, self-gratifying desire. It is sex driven primarily by desire, and conducted (whether in the head or with the body) for the good of self, not the other. Lust prioritizes personal pleasure, and holds back from making a personal commitment. It aims to give only in order to get. It serves only as an investment, to reap the dividend.

And this arises from a lack of knowledge of the God of the Bible. He is a God of holy compassion; the pagan (Gentile) gods were not. They demanded you did something for them before they would do something to bless you. You expected to serve them in order for them to save you. You gave in order to get.

So Paul is saying two surprising things. First, you can be sexually immoral while having sex within marriage, if you are driven by passionate lust, not holy love. Second, your attitude toward sex will reveal your true attitude toward God.

Q: *How do you react to those two statements? How do they (re)shape your view of how to be sexually moral?*

PRAY: *Pray that in a world driven by lust, you would know how to live in holy love. Amen.*

Day 5

1 THESSALONIANS 4:6-8

Q: *What scene might the start of v 6 picture?*

Nothing sinks a church faster than sexual immorality within it. Ironically, the closer and warmer a church family is—the *better* it is—the greater the danger of becoming *too* close and being burned. Sexual immorality has always been one of Satan's favorite weapons against God's people (read Numbers 25:1-3)

Q: *What warning does Paul then give (v 6)?*

God calls sinners, but he does not call us to remain in sin (v 7). He calls us to become like him, not to stay as we are.

Q: *How does verse 8 underline the seriousness of living God's way when it comes to sex and relationships?*

As Western cultures turn away from viewing sex from a biblical standpoint, the temptation to compromise will grow greater. It is natural to want to fit in. But we must ask: who knows best—man or God? Who can we more safely disregard—man, who does not know what will happen tomorrow, or God, who knows everything about every tomorrow? We are wearing clothes several sizes too big when we presume to tell God he should think more like us when it comes to sexual morality.

Q: *How are you most tempted to do this? What would it mean to please God when you are tempted in this way?*

PRAY: *Ask God, by his indwelling Spirit, to grant purity in your church family, and wisdom in seeing temptations to compromise.*

Day 6

1 THESSALONIANS 4:9-12

Q: *What type of love does Paul turn to speak of in verse 9?*

Q: *Where do Christians learn about this kind of love (v 9)?*

Q: *How are the Thessalonian Christians measuring up (v 10)? What should they now do (v 10)?*

For every danger in the Christian life, there is an equal and opposite error. Having warned this church to beware warm friendship becoming burning immorality, Paul also encourages them not to run to the other extreme—not to stop loving each other as a family. In an effort to avoid immorality, we are not to grow cold and distant toward one another. In fact, we are to love each other in this familial way "more and more" (v 10). And we learn how to love like this from God himself—the Father who loves his children enough to redeem them, the Son who loves his brothers and sisters enough to die for them, the Spirit who loves his people enough to dwell with them. That is the love God seeks in his people; the love that both pleases him (v 1) and makes an impression on outsiders (v 12).

Q: *How can you personally pursue this kind of love toward, and allow yourself to receive this kind of love from, others in your church? Be specific.*

Q: *Re-read v 1-12. How has the Spirit both excited you and called you to change?*

PRAY: *Speak to your holy, loving Father now about how his Spirit is calling you to live.*

JOURNAL

What I've learned or been particularly struck by this week…

_____
_____
_____
_____
_____
_____

What I want to change in my perspectives or actions as a result of this week…

_____
_____
_____
_____
_____
_____

Things I would like to think about more or discuss with others at my church…

_____
_____
_____
_____
_____
_____

BIBLE STUDY

Discuss

Have you ever had to break some bad news to someone, or tell them something that would be hard for them to hear? What fears did you have beforehand, and what was their reaction?

In this Bible study, we are going to look at how Paul viewed his approach to telling the truth to others. Paul is writing to the Christians in Thessalonica, whose church was born in troubled circumstances…

READ 1 THESSALONIANS 2:1-12

¹ For you yourselves know, brothers, that our coming to you was not in vain. ² But though we had already suffered and been shamefully treated at Philippi, as you know, we had boldness in our God to declare to you the gospel of God in the midst of much conflict.

1. What kind of reception had Paul been getting as he traveled around talking about the gospel? (See also Acts 17:1-15.)

But what is his assessment of his mission? What is his reasoning for this?

---

2. What temptations are Paul and his friends clearly aware of as they travel around teaching others the truth about Christ?

3. Gospel truth is a message that is conveyed by words. But what else is involved that enables the message to be clearly heard (v 6-9)?

4. What are some of the "acceptable" messages we have for the world that flow from the gospel?

And what are some of the messages that might provoke hostility and debate?

5. So what might our temptation be as the opportunity arises for us to speak truth into our confused world?

How can we encourage ourselves to remain faithful and focused?

_____

_____

_____

_____

6. How important is it, do you think, to challenge public thinking about ethical and other issues in our society? What should we be focusing on?

_____

_____

_____

Why is it important to keep verse 8 so clearly in our minds when speaking with others?

_____

_____

_____

Apply

Pick one or two of the subjects below about which Christians will have something clear to say. Imagine that you are with friends for coffee, or standing by the water cooler at work, and the subject comes up. Work out how you might:

(1) express clearly and lovingly what Christians believe on this subject and why.

(2) humbly ask some questions of them that get deeper into the issue.

(3) make a clear distinction between what the Bible says for definite; and what it does not say, and what is therefore an area for discussion.

(4) simply show that this is part of a much bigger worldview which has a loving and just God at its center.

(5) take the conversation to Jesus.

Topics to consider:

- Adultery

- Alcohol

- Lying and gossip

- The prominent failure of a Christian leader

- Abortion

- Homosexuality and gay marriage

- What is the most important political priority for our government?

Pray

FOR YOURSELF: Ask God to help you know the truth more clearly, and be able to speak about it humbly and faithfully. Pray that you would help others to think clearly about how to communicate gospel truths in a loving and compassionate way.

FOR YOUR CHURCH: Pray that your church would be obedient to Jesus' commands to not judge others, gossip, lie or be insulting. Pray that you would be a church marked by loving truthfulness and clarity.

SERMON NOTES

Bible passage: Date:

SESSION 6:

A JOYFUL CHURCH

IN A SUFFERING WORLD

WE LEARN MORE ABOUT OURSELVES AND ABOUT
OUR FAITH IN OUR SAVIOR IN PERIODS OF SUFFERING
THAN AT ANY OTHER TIME IN OUR LIVES. AND SINCE
WE LIVE IN A BROKEN WORLD, TO LIVE WITH JOY IN
HARDSHIPS IS A GREAT WITNESS TO THOSE AROUND
US. BUT THIS IS EASIER TO SAY THAN TO DO. HOW
CAN WE TRULY LIVE WITH HEARTFELT JOY WHEN LIFE
IS FALLING APART? AND HOW CAN WE HELP OTHERS
IN OUR CHURCHES TO DO THIS?

A JOYFUL CHURCH IN A SUFFERING WORLD

▶ WATCH DVD 6.1 OR LISTEN TO TALK 6.1

Discuss

Do you recognize the descriptions of the way people react to different kinds of suffering? How have you seen these in yourself and others?

Have you ever known someone who has "suffered well"? What impressed you about them?

_____

_____

_____

_____

_____

▶ WATCH DVD 6.2 OR LISTEN TO TALK 6.2

_____

_____

_____

_____

_____

_____

_____

_____

_____

_____

_____

👉 **HABAKKUK 3:17-19**

17 Though the fig tree should not blossom,
 nor fruit be on the vines,
the produce of the olive fail
 and the fields yield no food,
the flock be cut off from the fold
 and there be no herd in the stalls,

¹⁸ yet I will rejoice in the LORD;
  I will take joy in the God of my salvation.
¹⁹ God, the Lord, is my strength;
  he makes my feet like the deer's;
  he makes me tread on my high places.

  To the choirmaster: with stringed instruments.

Discuss

The circumstances that Habakkuk faces have not changed and yet he says that he is rejoicing. Why (v 18)?

What does Habakkuk know about God that makes it possible for him to rejoice (v 18-19)?

What do you think it means to have joy in suffering?

▶ WATCH DVD 6.3 OR LISTEN TO TALK 6.3

_____

_____

_____

_____

_____

_____

_____

_____

Discuss

How could you answer the following in a way that points to both God's goodness and sovereignty?

● "If you are suffering, you should pray to God and he will heal you."

_____

_____

● "If God doesn't heal you, it's because you don't trust him enough."

_____

_____

● "When life is hard, all you can do is grit your teeth and try to get through it."

_____

_____

● "If God loves me, why did I lose my job?"

_____

_____

- "If you are suffering, it must be because of some unconfessed sin in your life."

- "It's amazing how you keep going, even in such pain. I wish I had your faith."

What are some of the things we do in our church family that are unhelpful and discouraging for people who are suffering?

How do your answers show how to be helpful and supportive instead?

Pray

"Suffering is unbearable if you aren't certain that God is for you and with you." (Tim Keller, *Walking with God Through Pain and Suffering*)

Spend some time praising God for his love and sovereign care.

Ask him to help you to "suffer well" as you trust in his goodness.

Pray for any you know who are particularly struggling with suffering at the moment. Ask God to help you know how best to love and support them, and to point them to his goodness.

DAILY BIBLE DEVOTIONALS

When suffering comes, there is much we do not know and cannot understand. But in Romans 8, Paul gives us six great truths that we can know for sure, and cling on to.

Day 1

ROMANS 8:1-13

Q: *What does not exist, and who for (v 1)?*

Q: *What have we been set free from (v 2)?*

When a Christian suffers, it cannot be as a result of punishment by God. Why? Because God has already "condemned sin in the flesh" (v 3). The punishment for our sin has already fallen on someone else—on Jesus. He has taken the condemnation of all who are "in Christ Jesus" (v 1). Whatever trials you face in your life, it cannot be that God is punishing you.

Q: *What should someone who is "in Christ" now do (v 5-6)?*

Our character and reactions are shaped by what we think about. To set our minds on "the things of the Spirit" means to consciously bring to mind truths the Spirit wants to point us to. If we are to defeat sin… and if we would be joyful in suffering… we need these truths to be at the forefront of our thoughts, so that we see our lives in light of them.

Q: *What can someone who is "in Christ" look forward to (v 11)?*

PRAY: *Lord, thank you that in Christ, whatever comes, it will never be condemnation.*

Day 2

ROMANS 8:14-17

If we are "in Christ," his Spirit is in us (v 1, 9).

Q: *What is our relationship to God (v 14)?*

All that God's Son enjoys, we enjoy through faith in him. Tim Keller identifies six privileges of divine adoption in *Romans 8 – 16 For You*:

- Security (v 15a): we are adopted, and so we cannot lose our relationship with God.
- Authority (v 15a): we are sons, not slaves—members of creation's royal family. We know the One who owns the world is our Father.
- Intimacy (v 15b): we call the Creator of every atom "Abba"—he is our Daddy. We approach the King of everything and know that he loves us as his children.
- Assurance (v 16): we know in our spirit that we trust Christ—God's Spirit confirms in us this sense that yes, God is our loving Father.
- Inheritance (v 17): we stand to inherit and enjoy all that is God's, sharing his glory.
- Family likeness (v 17): we get to be like Christ—in suffering now, in glory later.

Q: *How do each of these privileges, flowing from our status as adopted children of God, help us when we face suffering?*

PRAY: *Father… thank you that I can call you that. Thank you that I am your child, and for all that means for me today and eternally.*

Day 3

ROMANS 8:18-25

Q: *What does Paul assume Christians will face in "this present time" (v 18)?*

Q: *Is our faith worth it, then? Why (v 18)?*

Christianity is not a ticket out of suffering in this life; but it is a way through that suffering. It is always worth it, because of what lies ahead. Paul now focuses on that future…

Q: *What does he say creation:*
  - *is doing in the present (v 19, 22)?*
  - *had done to it in the past (v 20)?*
  - *will enjoy in the future (v 21)?*

We are being given a (very brief!) "History of Creation." This world was made—it is a design, not an accident. This world was frustrated—it is not as it could be or should be. This world will be restored—free, glorious, all that it longs for, and that we long it to be.

When will this happen? At "the revealing of the sons of God" (v 19)—when God brings us home, to a home fit for him and his family—a perfect creation. This is the future God's children—you and I—can look forward to; where we are heading. So, Paul says, we are right to sense that suffering is an unnatural intrusion into this creation. We are to be realistic that every experience in our present will be tainted by some form of suffering. And we are to be hope-filled, because our future is glorious!

Q: *How should we wait (v 23, 25)?*

PRAY: *Father, thank you that you will bring me home. Make me eager for it when life goes well, and patient when life goes wrong.*

Day 4

When we suffer, we can remember our legal standing before God (v 1), our adoption into the family of God (v 14), and our future home with God (v 19, 21). Next, Paul says, we can have confidence to face trials because of who is with us in them.

ROMANS 8:26-27

Q: *What don't we know (v 26)? Have you experienced this in your own life?*

Q: *Who helps us, and how (v 26)?*

At those moments when we most need to pray to our *Abba*, we often find it hardest to know what to say. Wonderfully, when human words fail us, the language of the Spirit does not. We never need to feel that we cannot pray because we cannot find the words to say.

Q: *What does the Spirit do (v 27)?*

This is not an easy verse! Likely Paul is saying that, as we pray, the Spirit is saying to the Father: *If this child of yours knew you as well as I know you, and if this child of yours knew themself as well as I know them, this is what they'd say to you…* He takes our groans, our words and our thoughts and, when it's needed, turns them into a prayer pleasing to our Father.

In suffering we have the hope that we will be home with God in our future (v 23-25), and the assurance that God is with us in our present (v 26-27). Our Father is with us, in us and for us—no matter how hard the journey.

Q: *How are you prompted to pray today?*

PRAY: *Father, thank you that I can pray. Please, by your Spirit, help me to pray.*

Day 5

ROMANS 8:28-29

Q: *What do we know (v 28a)? Why is the word "all" crucial in this sentence?*

Q: *To whom is this promise made (v 28)?*

Q: *What has God decided his children will be (v 29)?*

Verse 29 tells us what the "good" of verse 28 actually is. It is to become more like our brother Jesus. God is always working—including in times of suffering—to make us as loving, courageous, compassionate, wise, gentle, passionate and peaceful as Jesus. We might define "good" as being our "comfort" or "convenience"—God defines it as Christ-likeness. And he uses our suffering, and all other circumstances of life, to achieve this end.

Q: *How does this transform our view of suffering? What does it cause us to ask when we face trials?*

Q: *Reflect on a period of suffering you have faced in your Christian life. Can you see ways God was using it to work for your good, making you more like Christ?*

Here is how we enjoy the good times of life without coming to rely on them; and how we face the hard times without being crushed by them. We know what is "good"—being more like Jesus, the perfect person. And we know that God is working for it—whether or not we can, in that moment, see how.

PRAY: *Father, please work for my Christ-likeness, rather than my comfort. And help me to want the former more than the latter.*

Day 6

ROMANS 8:30-39

Q: *What has God done for his people (v 30)?*

The tense of the final verb is astonishing—because it has not yet happened! But it is so certain that it can be spoken of as though it has already taken place. If God has worked in eternity past to foreknow and predestine you, and in your life to bring you to justifying faith in Christ, he *will* bring you to glory in your future.

Q: *How do we know God is for us today, and will give us all we need (v 32)?*

Q: *What scenarios does Paul imagine might convince us that we're not truly loved by Jesus (v 35-36)?*

Q: *What is Paul's answer (v 37-39)?*

The reason we find suffering so hard is because it causes us to question whether we are truly loved by God. *Can he really love me, if he lets this happen?* we ask. Paul answers: *Yes! In his love God does not bring you around suffering, but through it—and he uses that suffering for your good. He gave his Son to you—he will give you all you need to conquer your trials as your faith survives, and even grows, through them. Yes, he loves you!*

So, here is what we cling to as we suffer. We are not being condemned. We are God's children. We have a glorious future. We can pray with the Spirit's help. God is using it to make us more like Jesus. And nothing—*nothing*—will stop him loving us, into eternity.

PRAY: *Turn each truth into praise to God, and pray that you will cling to it in trials.*

JOURNAL

What I've learned or been particularly struck by this week…

_____
_____
_____
_____
_____
_____

What I want to change in my perspectives or actions as a result of this week…

_____
_____
_____
_____
_____
_____

Things I would like to think about more or discuss with others at my church…

_____
_____
_____
_____
_____
_____

JOURNAL

BIBLE STUDY

Discuss

Have you ever had a time in your Christian life when you have doubted God because of suffering? Why does the question of God's love and the existence of suffering remain one of the greatest difficulties for believing in God?

READ HEBREWS 11:1-3, 32-40

¹ Now faith is the assurance of things hoped for, the conviction of things not seen. ² For by it the people of old received their commendation. ³ By faith we understand that the universe was created by the word of God, so that what is seen was not made out of things that are visible.

In this famous passage we see how the good news of the gospel leads to people who are united in Christ and willing to follow his example of sacrificial service.

1. What picture do these verses present of what we should expect the "normal" Christian life to be like?

_____

_____

_____

_____

2. What enabled these believers to face both triumphs and suffering, and still maintain their trust in God (v 32-40; see also v 1)?

_____

_____

_____

_____

3. What are believers tempted to think when we face suffering?

How would remembering the experience of these "heroes of the faith" have helped the Hebrew Christians as they faced persecution?

READ HEBREWS 12:1-3

[1] *Therefore, since we are surrounded by so great a cloud of witnesses, let us also lay aside every weight, and sin which clings so closely, and let us run with endurance the race that is set before us.*

4. What should we do as a result of meditating on the experiences of our Old Testament brothers and sisters?

5. Why should the example and work of Jesus Christ give us so much more confidence as we face suffering and persecution?

What will it mean in practice for us to look to—or fix our eyes on—Jesus (v 2)?

_____

_____

_____

6. This is not a quick fix. Suffering and persecution can last for years. What are the twin dangers we face when suffering of any kind persists (v 3)? How can we help ourselves and each other not to succumb to these temptations?

_____

_____

_____

Apply

FOR YOURSELF: What do you think are the things that hinder and entangle you so that you are not running the race well? Do you think your faith is strong enough to withstand—and even flourish in the face of—physical, emotional or relational suffering, or even persecution?

_____

_____

_____

FOR YOUR CHURCH: Does your church have a culture of honesty where people can share how they are struggling—or is there a general feeling that everyone is coping and doing well? How might you be part of the way in which your church becomes a more nurturing place for people who may be suffering in silence at the moment?

_____

_____

_____

Pray

FOR YOUR GROUP: Spend some time praising your Savior for his perseverance in the face of ultimate suffering. Pray for each other—that God would prepare you for the suffering that will inevitably face us all at some time.

FOR YOUR CHURCH: Pray that your preaching and conversation would encourage people to look to Jesus. Pray that those who are suffering in silence might be encouraged to seek help and support from their brothers and sisters.

FOR THE CHURCH THROUGHOUT THE WORLD: Many of our brothers and sisters worldwide are facing hostile opposition every day. Pray that those who are persecuted would continue to trust Jesus; that they would look to him, and persevere to his praise and glory.

SERMON NOTES

Bible passage: Date:

SESSION 7:

HOW TO BE THE CHURCH IN THE WORLD

THE CALLING OF YOUR CHURCH – TO SHINE GOD'S LIGHT IN A DARK PLACE – IS A GREAT ONE, BUT ALSO AN INTIMIDATING ONE. BUT GOD DOES NOT LEAVE US ALONE IN THIS. IN THIS FINAL SESSION, WE WILL CONSIDER HOW HIS SPIRIT IS WORKING IN, THROUGH AND AROUND US, ENABLING US TO BE THE PEOPLE OUR FATHER HAS CALLED US TO BE, FOR HIS GLORY AND FOR THE GOOD OF HIS WORLD.

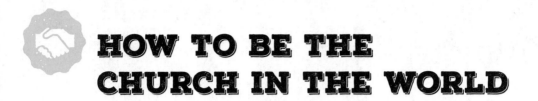

HOW TO BE THE CHURCH IN THE WORLD

▶ WATCH DVD 7.1 OR LISTEN TO TALK 7.1

Discuss

Did the DVD/talk ring true for you? Do you feel swamped and inadequate to be God's light in the world? How?

WATCH DVD 7.2 OR LISTEN TO TALK 7.2

GALATIANS 5:16-17, 25

¹⁶ But I say, walk by the Spirit, and you will not gratify the desires of the flesh. ¹⁷ For the desires of the flesh are against the Spirit, and the desires of the Spirit are against the flesh, for these are opposed to each other, to keep you from doing the things you want to do.

²⁵ If we live by the Spirit, let us also keep in step with the Spirit.

Discuss

In verse 25, "live by the Spirit" means that we have already been brought to life by the Holy Spirit as we responded to the gospel message. So what do you think Paul is encouraging the Galatians to do when he tells them to "walk by the Spirit" and "keep in step with the Spirit"?

"We cannot expect to be lights for God in the world if following God is not an active, ongoing commitment that we are daily pursuing." What will this look like in your life? And in the life of your church family?

_____

_____

_____

_____

_____

▶ **WATCH DVD 7.3 OR LISTEN TO TALK 7.3**

_____

_____

_____

_____

_____

_____

_____

_____

_____

_____

_____

GALATIANS 6:1-3

[1] *Brothers, if anyone is caught in any transgression, you who are spiritual should restore him in a spirit of gentleness. Keep watch on yourself, lest you too be tempted.* [2] *Bear one another's burdens, and so fulfill the law of Christ.* [3] *For if anyone thinks he is something, when he is nothing, he deceives himself.*

Discuss

"The church community should be the safest place to be when we fail." Why should this be true, according to Galatians 6? Have you ever experienced restoration after failure, or seen it in your church family?

_____

_____

_____

_____

_____

_____

_____

"As a fellowship, we can face the things that might otherwise overwhelm and discourage us, because we don't face them alone." Can you think of some ways in which you can support others in your church family practically, emotionally and spiritually?

_____

_____

_____

_____

_____

_____

_____

Look back over your notes and journal from the previous sessions.

- What are some of the things you have been challenged to do as an individual so that you shine more brightly (= are more like Jesus) in a dark world?

_____

_____

_____

_____

_____

- What are some of the changes you could make as a church family to be a brighter, more effective light in your neighborhood?

_____

_____

_____

_____

_____

_____

Pray

GALATIANS 5:22-23

22 But the fruit of the Spirit is love, joy, peace, patience, kindness, goodness, faithfulness, 23 gentleness, self-control.

Ask God to work in you by his Spirit so that you grow in these qualities.

Look at some of the practical things you have written on this page. Pray that you will be able to put these into practice to shine brightly in the world.

DAILY BIBLE DEVOTIONALS

Our calling as churches is to shine Christ's light in the world. That's exhilarating—and intimidating! Here, we study the church in Acts, seeing how we really can shine bright.

Day 1

ACTS 2:42-47

This church had been formed through Peter's gospel sermon at Pentecost, which had resulted in 3,000 conversions (v 41).

Q: *What did these new Christians do as they met together (v 42)?*

Q: *When did they meet and where (v 46)?*

Q: *What word does Luke use to describe their attitude to their church (v 42)?*

When another church grows fast, we tend to search for the "church-growth silver bullet" that they have clearly found. Here we find a rapidly growing church (v 47), so let us learn from them… but Acts 2 gives us no new program or six-step process toward mega-church size. No—we are pointed to their commitment (day by day they met); their practice (gospel teaching in gospel fellowship); their openness (they met publicly as well as behind closed doors); and perhaps most of all, their attitude—devotion. As you rely on God to work through you (v 43, 47), your church can do all this! But will you? And what part will you play?

Q: *Would "devoted" describe your attitude toward your church? Why/why not?*

PRAY: *Ask for true devotion to your church.*

Day 2

ACTS 4:23-31

All through Acts, gospel growth triggers persecution. In these verses, the church is meeting after Peter and John are told by the courts to stop evangelizing.

Q: *What do they do (v 24)?*

Q: *What do they ask for (v 29-30)?*

Your church will never, in its own strength, be the church God calls you to be. But wonderfully, it does not need to be; God stands ready to make you the church he calls you to be. Notice how the Lord answers the prayers of this new, young, outnumbered, threatened church (v 31). If we want to be lights in the world, we must ask for assistance from the King of the world. A church that truly shines in the world will be a praying church. Self-reliance never grows a fellowship. We, like this church in Acts 4, have all of heaven's power at our disposal. But do we ask for it?

Q: *Are you praying regularly for your church's witness? Does your church have prayer meetings… and do you turn up?*

Q: *Read Ephesians 3:20-21. How does this excite you to pray for your church?!*

PRAY: *Thank God for ruling; for speaking; for listening; and for working through his people.*

Day 3

ACTS 4:32-37

We saw in 2:44-45 that "all who believed were together and had all things in common," including their possessions and wealth.

Q: *How do we see that happening in more detail in these verses?*

Do not miss the magnitude of what is going on here, and its challenging implications for us. These Christians shared *everything*, not considering anything as "mine" but treating it as "ours." These Christians sold their houses so that there would be no one in their church who was in need.

Would we ever do these things to this extent? Imagine what a wonderful community, and a powerful witness, it would be if we did. What stops us thinking of things as "mine" and ring-fencing our houses, pension plans and so on? Appreciating that "great grace [is] upon" us (v 33). It is understanding and relying on God's generosity—the grace that comes to us from the risen Jesus—that enables us to be radically generous with all he's given us.

Q: *In what ways are you personally, and your church as a whole, reflecting the generosity we see in these verses?*

Q: *Are there ways in which your attitude to your church and "your" possessions is challenged by the church in Acts? Any specific changes you need to make?*

PRAY: *Spend time thanking God for his grace to you. Then pray that any changes he has laid on your heart to make would translate into real actions.*

Day 4

ACTS 6:1-7

Q: *What is happening to this church at the start and end of this episode (v 1a, 7)?*

Q: *But what is the problem (v 1)?*

Q: *What wrong solution is rejected (v 2)? What solution is decided upon (v 3, 5-6)?*

If the apostles had stopped teaching God's word, the church would have become a soup kitchen. Soup kitchens are great, and necessary; but they do not serve eternal life. Equally, if the apostles had not made sure that the church provided for physical needs as well as for spiritual ones, mercy would have been taught, but not lived out. Instead, this church prioritized both; the apostles focused on word ministry while appointing deacons to focus on mercy ministry. Both are vital; neither are optional.

This is how the church provides a picture of the eternal kingdom of God—a place of truth and provision. It was what Israel had been meant to do (Deuteronomy 15:4-5), but failed to—here, the church succeeds. This may explain why "a great many of the priests" are converted at this point (Acts 6:7)—they see God's kingdom in the church. Our light shines brightest when we both teach truth *and* live mercifully.

Q: *Does your church provide for, promote and pray about both these ministries?*

Q: *What part do you/could you play in gospel teaching and/or gospel caring?*

PRAY: *Pray that your church will teach truth and wait on tables—and that this will build up Christians and attract non-Christians.*

Day 5

Being a deacon does not mean that someone does no gospel teaching. And one deacon, Stephen, ends up being condemned to death for his witness to Christ in court…

ACTS 7:54 – 8:8

Q: *What happens to Stephen, and to the church (7:59 – 8:3)?*

Q: *Homeless… scattered… in danger… How do these Christians respond (v 4-5)?*

Q: *What had the persecution achieved?!*

As Western societies become increasingly post-Christian and governments pass laws that are anti-Christian, we naturally worry that our mission will be thwarted and our churches will decline. We need the Acts church to teach us to view setbacks as opportunities. The darkest nights are the ones when lights can shine brightest. Jesus has promised that "the gates of hell shall not prevail" against his church (Matt. 16:18)—he has kept that promise through the centuries, and he will keep it today. Opposition and persecution may come, but it does not mean the church will fail; nor is it an excuse for faltering. We do not choose opposition or welcome persecution— but we must see them as opportunities, and ask Christ to use them, and use us in them.

Q: *How does this change your attitude to trends in your culture?*

Q: *How does it both comfort and challenge you, personally and for your church?*

PRAY: *Ask that you will not see opposition as a defeat, but as an opportunity.*

Day 6

ACTS 11:19-26

One of the consequences of the Jerusalem persecution was the planting of a church in Antioch—a Jew-only church (v 19)…

Q: *What happened next (v 20-21—Hellenists means Greeks, or non-Jews)?*

The truth that the gospel was as much for Gentiles as Jews had only been recently discovered (10:44 – 11:18)—so Barnabas was sent to see what was happening (v 22).

Q: *How did he react, what did he exhort, and what was the result (v 23-24)?*

Q: *What term was first used there (v 26)?*

This word is so familiar that we rarely stop to think about it. It was not necessarily used as a compliment—but it reveals how this church was viewed. It describes both identity and personal loyalty. A "Herodian" was a follower of Herod, loyal to him and serving his cause. A Christian is a follower of King Jesus, loyal to him, serving his cause. If we are to deserve the name Christian, people must see not our church-attending and morals-keeping so much as our unswerving devotion to our sovereign.

Q: *Is this how you, and your church, are known by unbelievers?*

The churches in Acts grew thrillingly. Their lights shone brightly. Ours can and must, too.

Q: *Reflect on this week's devotionals. How have they excited and challenged you about how God might use you today?*

PRAY: *Turn your answers into prayers.*

JOURNAL

What I've learned or been particularly struck by this week...

_____
_____
_____
_____
_____
_____

What I want to change in my perspectives or actions as a result of this week...

_____
_____
_____
_____
_____
_____

Things I would like to think about more or discuss with others at my church...

_____
_____
_____
_____
_____
_____

BIBLE STUDY

Discuss

Have you ever spoken with someone who has been "put off" Jesus because of the way they were badly treated at church or by Christians? What mistakes were made, and how could they have been corrected?

READ GALATIANS 5:25 – 6:10

25 If we live by the Spirit, let us also keep in step with the Spirit...

Paul is speaking to an issue we all feel very deeply—the gap between who God has made us in Christ, and what our current lives are really like. We are not what we were, and we are not what we will be in the new creation. But now, in the "in-between times," we can still be ruled by our sinful desires, rather than by the Holy Spirit. We have been made alive by the Holy Spirit as we responded to the gospel message ("we live by the Spirit," v 25), but now we need consciously and deliberately to "keep in step with the Spirit."

1. The phrase "keep in step with the Spirit" is a military metaphor—bringing to mind a marching army. What does this image imply about the way we should live as believers? Why does Paul mention the particular things he does in verse 26?

2. What are some bad ways churches might respond to an individual's personal, moral or spiritual failure? By contrast, how does the gospel urge us to deal with this problem (v 1-3)?

Apply

3. Which of these responses to failure have you seen happen in your church fellowship? How could you as an individual help improve on this?

_____

_____

_____

_____

4. What is the principle in verses 7-8, and how does this help us in our struggle to grow in godliness?

_____

_____

_____

_____

5. What does Paul encourage us to do in verses 9 and 10, and what does that involve?

_____

_____

_____

_____

What motivations and priorities are there for being like this?

_____

_____

_____

_____

6. Why is it easy for us to "grow weary of doing good"? How can we combat love fatigue?

_____

_____

_____

_____

Review

YOURSELF: Look back together over what we have looked at in these seven sessions. What did you find particularly challenging? How can you maintain your own growth in godliness as an individual and as part of the congregation?

_____

_____

_____

YOUR CHURCH: What does your church struggle most with, do you think? Growing in a holy, gracious and vibrant Christian life; or showing that life attractively and compellingly to a world that is hungry for authentic, truthful and loving relationships?

_____

_____

_____

Pray

FOR YOUR GROUP: Ask the Lord to help you be honest about your own weaknesses and failures with each other, and that you would deal with each other gently and lovingly.

FOR YOUR CHURCH: Pray that your leaders would help you grow in godliness and in being an effective witness in the world.

SERMON NOTES

Bible passage: Date:

GOSPEL SHAPED

CHURCH

The Complete Series

LET THE POWER OF THE GOSPEL SHAPE FOUR OTHER CRITICAL AREAS IN THE LIFE OF YOUR CHURCH

"WE WANT CHURCHES CALLED INTO EXISTENCE BY THE GOSPEL TO BE SHAPED BY THE GOSPEL IN THEIR EVERYDAY LIFE."

DON CARSON AND TIM KELLER

GOSPEL SHAPED
WORSHIP

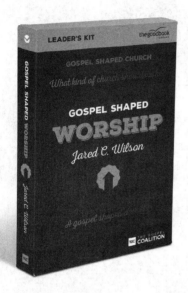

Christians are people who have discovered that the one true object of our worship is the God who has revealed himself in and through Jesus Christ.

But what exactly is worship? What should we be doing when we meet together for "church" on Sundays? And how does that connect with what we do the rest of the week?

This seven-week whole-church curriculum explores what it means to be a worshiping community. As we search the Scriptures together, we will discover that true worship must encompass the whole of life. This engaging and flexible resource will challenge us to worship God every day of the week, with all our heart, mind, soul and strength.

Written and presented by **JARED C. WILSON**
Jared is Director of Communications at Midwestern Seminary and College in Kansas City, and a prolific author. He is married to Becky and has two daughters.

WWW.GOSPELSHAPEDCHURCH.ORG/WORSHIP

GOSPEL SHAPED
OUTREACH

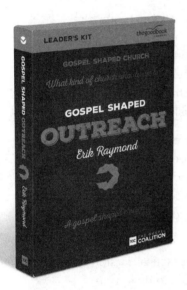

Many Christians are nervous about telling someone else about Jesus. The nine sessions in this curriculum don't offer quick fixes or evangelism "gimmicks." But by continually pointing us back to the gospel, they will give us the proper motivation to work together as a church to share the gospel message with those who are lost without Christ.

As you work through the material, you will discover that God's mission of salvation in the world is also your mission; and that he is inviting you into the privilege of praying and working to advance his kingdom among your family, friends, neighbors, co-workers and community.

Gospel Shaped Church is a new curriculum from The Gospel Coalition that will help whole congregations pause and think slowly, carefully and prayerfully about the kind of church they are called to be.

Written and presented by **ERIK RAYMOND**
Erik is the Preaching Pastor at Emmaus Bible Church in Omaha, Nebraska. He is married to Christie and has six children.

WWW.GOSPELSHAPEDCHURCH.ORG/OUTREACH

GOSPEL SHAPED
WORK

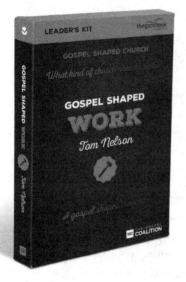

Many Christians experience a troubling disconnect between their everyday work and what they live and work for as a believer in Jesus. How should the gospel shape my view of life on an assembly line, or change my work as a teacher, artist, nurse, home-maker or gardener?

Gospel Shaped Work explores over eight sessions how the gospel changes the way we view our work in the world—and how a church should equip its members to serve God in their everyday vocations, and relate to the wider world of work and culture.

These engaging and practical sessions are designed to reveal the Bible's all-encompassing vision for our daily lives, and our engagement with culture as a redeemed community. They will provoke a fresh discussion in your church about how the gospel of Christ impacts every area of life in our world.

Written and presented by **TOM NELSON**
Tom is the Senior Pastor of Christ Community Church in Kansas City, and a council member of The Gospel Coalition. He is married to Liz and has two grown children.

WWW.GOSPELSHAPEDCHURCH.ORG/WORK

"THESE RESOURCES GIVE SPACE TO CONSIDER WHAT A GENUINE EXPRESSION OF A GOSPEL-SHAPED CHURCH LOOKS LIKE FOR YOU IN THE PLACE GOD HAS PUT YOU, AND WITH THE PEOPLE HE HAS GATHERED INTO FELLOWSHIP WITH YOU."

DON CARSON AND TIM KELLER

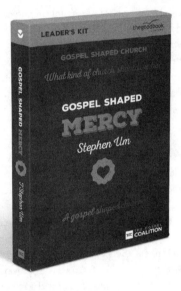

GOSPEL SHAPED
MERCY

The gospel is all about justice and mercy: the just punishment of God falling on his Son, Jesus, so that he can have mercy on me, a sinner.

But many churches have avoided following through on the Bible's clear teaching on working for justice and mercy in the wider world. They fear that it is a distraction from the primary task of gospel preaching.

This *Gospel Shaped Mercy* module explores how individual Christians and whole churches can and should be engaged in the relief of poverty, hunger and injustice in a way that adorns the gospel of grace.

Written and presented by **STEPHEN UM**
Stephen is Senior Minister of Citylife Church in Boston, MA, and is a council member of The Gospel Coalition.

WWW.GOSPELSHAPEDCHURCH.ORG/MERCY

THE GOSPEL
COALITION

This set of resources is based on the five principles of gospel-centered ministry as laid out in The Gospel Coalition's foundation documents. The text reads:

What is gospel–centered ministry?
It is characterized by:

1. Empowered corporate worship
The gospel changes our relationship with God from one of hostility or slavish compliance to one of intimacy and joy. The core dynamic of gospel–centered ministry is therefore worship and fervent prayer. In corporate worship God's people receive a special life–transforming sight of the worth and beauty of God, and then give back to God suitable expressions of his worth. At the heart of corporate worship is the ministry of the Word. Preaching should be expository (explaining the text of Scripture) and Christ–centered (expounding all biblical themes as climaxing in Christ and his work of salvation). Its ultimate goal, however, is not simply to teach but to lead the hearers to worship, individual and corporate, that strengthens their inner being to do the will of God.

2. Evangelistic effectiveness
Because the gospel (unlike religious moralism) produces people who do not disdain those who disagree with them, a truly gospel–centered church should be filled with members who winsomely address people's hopes and aspirations with Christ and his saving work. We have a vision for a church that sees conversions of rich and poor, highly educated and less educated, men and women, old and young, married and single, and all races. We hope to draw highly secular and postmodern people, as well as reaching religious and traditional people. Because of the attractiveness of its community and the humility of its people, a gospel–centered

church should find people in its midst who are exploring and trying to understand Christianity. It must welcome them in hundreds of ways. It will do little to make them "comfortable" but will do much to make its message understandable. In addition to all this, gospel–centered churches will have a bias toward church planting as one of the most effective means of evangelism there is.

3. Counter–cultural community
Because the gospel removes both fear and pride, people should get along inside the church who could never get along outside. Because it points us to a man who died for his enemies, the gospel creates relationships of service rather than of selfishness. Because the gospel calls us to holiness, the people of God live in loving bonds of mutual accountability and discipline. Thus the gospel creates a human community radically different from any society around it. Regarding sex, the church should avoid both the secular society's idolization of sex and traditional society's fear of it. It is a community which so loves and cares practically for its members that biblical chastity makes sense. It teaches its members to conform their bodily being to the shape of the gospel—abstinence outside of heterosexual marriage and fidelity and joy within. Regarding the family, the church should affirm the goodness of marriage between a man and a woman, calling them to serve God by reflecting his covenant love in life–long loyalty, and by teaching his ways to their children. But it also affirms the goodness of serving Christ as singles, whether for a time or for a life. The church should surround all persons suffering from the fallenness of our human sexuality with a compassionate

community and family. Regarding money, the church's members should engage in radical economic sharing with one another—so "there are no needy among them" (Acts 4:34). Such sharing also promotes a radically generous commitment of time, money, relationships, and living space to social justice and the needs of the poor, the oppressed, the immigrant, and the economically and physically weak. Regarding power, it is visibly committed to power–sharing and relationship–building among races, classes, and generations that are alienated outside of the Body of Christ. The practical evidence of this is that our local churches increasingly welcome and embrace people of all races and cultures. Each church should seek to reflect the diversity of its local geographical community, both in the congregation at large and in its leadership.

4. The integration of faith and work

The good news of the Bible is not only individual forgiveness but the renewal of the whole creation. God put humanity in the garden to cultivate the material world for his own glory and for the flourishing of nature and the human community. The Spirit of God not only converts individuals (e.g., John 16:8) but also renews and cultivates the face of the earth (e.g., Gen 1:2; Psalm 104:30). Therefore Christians glorify God not only through the ministry of the Word, but also through their vocations of agriculture, art, business, government, scholarship—all for God's glory and the furtherance of the public good. Too many Christians have learned to seal off their faith–beliefs from the way they work in their vocation. The gospel is seen as a means of finding individual peace and not as the foundation of a worldview—a comprehensive interpretation of reality affecting all that we do. But we have a vision for a church that equips its people to think out the implications of the gospel on how we do carpentry, plumbing, data–entry, nursing, art, business, government, journalism, entertainment, and scholarship. Such a church will not only support Christians' engagement with culture, but will also help them work with distinctiveness, excellence, and accountability in their trades and professions. Developing humane yet creative and excellent business environments out of our understanding of the gospel is part of the work of bringing a measure of healing to God's creation in the power of the Spirit. Bringing Christian joy, hope, and truth to embodiment in the arts is also part of this work. We do all of this because the gospel of God leads us to it, even while we recognize that the ultimate restoration of all things awaits the personal and bodily return of our Lord Jesus Christ

5. The doing of justice and mercy

God created both soul and body, and the resurrection of Jesus shows that he is going to redeem both the spiritual and the material. Therefore God is concerned not only for the salvation of souls but also for the relief of poverty, hunger, and injustice. The gospel opens our eyes to the fact that all our wealth (even wealth for which we worked hard) is ultimately an unmerited gift from God. Therefore the person who does not generously give away his or her wealth to others is not merely lacking in compassion, but is unjust. Christ wins our salvation through losing, achieves power through weakness and service, and comes to wealth through giving all away. Those who receive his salvation are not the strong and accomplished but those who admit they are weak and lost. We cannot look at the poor and the oppressed and callously call them to pull themselves out of their own difficulty. Jesus did not treat us that way. The gospel replaces superiority toward the poor with mercy and compassion. Christian churches must work for justice and peace in their neighborhoods through service even as they call individuals to conversion and the new birth. We must work for the eternal and common good and show our neighbors we love them sacrificially whether they believe as we do or not. Indifference to the poor and disadvantaged means there has not been a true grasp of our salvation by sheer grace.

thegoodbook
COMPANY

Opening up the Bible

At The Good Book Company, we are dedicated to helping Christians and local churches grow. We believe that God's growth process always starts with hearing clearly what he has said to us through his timeless word—the Bible.

Ever since we opened our doors in 1991, we have been striving to produce resources that honor God in the way the Bible is used. We have grown to become an international provider of user-friendly resources to the Christian community, with believers of all backgrounds and denominations using our Bible studies, books, evangelistic resources, DVD-based courses and training events.

We want to equip ordinary Christians to live for Christ day by day, and churches to grow in their knowledge of God, their love for one another, and the effectiveness of their outreach.

Call us for a discussion of your needs or visit one of our local websites for more information on the resources and services we provide.

North America: www.thegoodbook.com
UK & Europe: www.thegoodbook.co.uk
Australia: www.thegoodbook.com.au
New Zealand: www.thegoodbook.co.nz

North America: 866 244 2165
UK & Europe: 0333 123 0880
Australia: (02) 6100 4211
New Zealand (+64) 3 343 2463